KANT'S PHILOSOPHICAL REVOLUTION

Kant's Philosophical Revolution

A SHORT GUIDE TO THE
CRITIQUE OF PURE REASON

Yirmiyahu Yovel

PRINCETON UNIVERSITY PRESS

PRINCETON & OXFORD

Requests for permission to reproduce material from this work
should be sent to Permissions, Princeton University Press

Published by Princeton University Press,
41 William Street, Princeton, New Jersey 08540

In the United Kingdom: Princeton University Press,
6 Oxford Street, Woodstock, Oxfordshire OX20 1TR

press.princeton.edu

Jacket art: Ornaments from the title page of the original 1781 edition
of the *Critik der reinen Vernunft* by Immanuel Kant

ISBN 978-0-691-18052-6

Library of Congress Control Number: 2017962524

British Library Cataloging-in-Publication Data is available

This book has been composed in Miller

Printed on acid-free paper. ∞

Printed in the United States of America

10 9 8 7 6 5 4 3 2 1

CONTENTS

Preface · ix

PERHAPS THE MOST influential book of philosophical modernity, Kant's *Critique of Pure Reason*, is also one of the hardest to read. Both in substance and in style it often makes the reader wonder where the argument goes, or how to understand a difficult idea or tortuous sentence. Not only was Kant a philosophical revolutionary, he also had to invent the language by which to express his innovative ideas; and in both ways he had to act as pathbreaker. (He was also writing fast, as if to beat a deadline.) No wonder the *Critique* was misunderstood from the start (which made Kant revise it in the second edition) and has been the object of diverging interpretations.

This short book is intended to help readers find their way through the web of Kant's classic. It is intended not as a defense, or evaluation, but as a descriptive explication. Leaving many secondary matters on the sidelines, I distilled the major issues and arguments and present them in the order in which they arise in the book. The result is an interpretation carried out by a systematic exposition.

The text is based on the introduction to my Hebrew translation of the *Critique of Pure Reason*, published with notes a few years ago in Tel-Aviv. This was a massive undertaking that, as often happens, claimed my time and dedicated energy far more than had been anticipated at the outset. Even the project's happy conclusion did not allow me the luxury of rest. Colleagues and students urged me to translate the text of the introduction into English as a stand-alone book, a systematic guide that provides both an overview of the whole *Critique* in context (as Kant insisted it should be treated) and an elucidation of the train of ideas and arguments through which Kant's philosophical revolution is carried out.

This work would never have taken off, let alone be concluded, without the determined and loving support of my wife, the writer Shoshana Yovel, who is my first reader and critic. I am also indebted to the many who encouraged me along the way with a cheerful reaction or wise comment, and created a mood of expectation that helped me persist. Most valuable was the input of talented and curious students of several generations who took part in my Kant seminars in Jerusalem and New York. Among my former assistants I thank in particular Pini Ifergan, Dror Yinon, Tal Kohavi, Gal Katz, and Ohad Reis.

Institutionally, I thank the Hebrew University of Jerusalem, my first academic home, and the New School for Social Research, New York, my second academic home, for providing a suitable environment for intellectual work. My friend Martin Gross of Livingston, New Jersey, was a frequent visitor in my seminars at the New School. A philosopher and businessman, Marty demonstrated a keen interest in my Kant project and provided a research grant to facilitate its progress. Thanks are also due to the German-Israeli Research Foundation (GIF) for financial and administrative support. And, as in most of my former books, Eva Shorr, Associate Editor of the Jerusalem Philosophical Quarterly IYYUN, was always available for intelligent consultation.

PART ONE

Preliminary Observations: Rethinking the Object

KANT MAINTAINS THAT every human advancement, especially in the sciences, originates in a revolution in the mode of thinking, which elevates a certain domain of knowledge to the level of an apodictic science. In the past, this had taken place in mathematics and physics, and now, after many centuries of groping in the dark, the conditions are ripe for a revolution that would signal the royal road also for philosophy.

The core of the philosophical revolution lies in a completely new understanding of the concept of object, or objective being, and its relation to human knowledge. Kant compares the required reversal to the one Copernicus performed in astronomy. Until Copernicus, the earth was seen as fixed in the center and the sun as revolving around it. Copernicus made us see that, on the contrary, the sun stands in the center while the earth revolves around it. Similarly, philosophers since ancient times believed that human knowledge revolves around the object, that is, must fit the structure and features of an object that stands in itself independently from the outset, and does not depend on the process of knowledge. The Kantian revolution abolishes the object's metaphysical independence and makes it dependent on the structure of human knowledge. The structure of the object—meaning the empirical object, the only one we know—is derived a priori (free of sense-experience) from the human understanding (intellect) that connects a multitude of sensible items into a unity; and the modes of this unification are drawn from the primordial unity of the "I think." Kant's bold idea thus says that the understanding, in knowing the world, does not copy the basic patterns of its knowledge from the world, but rather *dictates* these patterns to the world. Doing so is a condition for the very existence of an empirical world ruled by necessary laws (which alone deserves the title "objective"), and for the existence of real objects and events in it.

This means not that the human understanding creates the world ex nihilo, but that it constitutes a cosmos from chaos. The understanding is a formal, a priori structure that cannot function without the material we acquire from the senses by being passively exposed to them. The senses supply the understanding with a crude element that is not yet a real object but only the material for it; and the understanding, a spontaneous factor, must order and shape this material according to its (the understanding's) own a priori modes of operation.

This implies that objectivity is a status that is *constituted* rather than immediately given or passively encountered. When the understanding applies its a priori patterns, called "categories," to the sensible material, it creates an objective synthesis between them. It is this objective synthesis that constitutes the empirical entities and states of affairs that deserve being called real or objective. As such, the concepts "object," "objectivity," and "empirical reality" acquire a radically new philosophical interpretation.

At the background of this doctrine stands the recognition that all the contents of our thinking and perception are mental images (called "ideas" by Descartes and Hume, and "representations" [*Vorstellungen*] by Kant) and never things beyond the mind. Humans have no way of leaping outside the sphere of the mental and hold on to something that lies in itself beyond their representations. Therefore, even such features as permanence and substantiality, and the rest of the necessary relations that build up an objective state of affairs, must be drawn *from the mind itself*—in its function as intellect.

Few would deny that an objective state of affairs lays down a normative model to which, in order to be true, all our cognitive propositions must correspond while also agreeing among themselves.[1] This is a nominal feature of truth; and the question is how the correspondence is achieved. The prevailing metaphysical realism maintains that objective states of affairs exist in themselves, outside the mind, which must adjust its representations to them; whereas Kant reverses this order in stating it is the mind itself that endows the representations with the unity, the permanence, and the necessary relations by which the objective state of affairs (in short, the object) is constituted.

The Foundations of the Sciences

The question about the object takes in Kant also the form of the question about *the foundations of mathematics and the natural sciences*: what makes their validity possible? The two issues converge because it is on the scientific level of knowledge that the synthesis of the sensual materials that constitutes an object is carried out. For this reason—and also because of the historical context—the question about the natural sciences and the question about the object are two faces of the same investigation by which Kant sought to create a critical metaphysics. Many English-speaking interpreters, as well as neo-Kantian German scholars, tended to present the issue from the viewpoint of the natural sciences, and thereby reduced Kant's philosophical innovation to epistemology and the validity of science. The present study prefers the standpoint of the object, in order to highlight the Critique's broader philosophical meaning (and role in modern thinking), which concerns the human being's standing in the

---

1. That is, every true proposition (judgment) regarding the object should agree with every other true proposition regarding the same object.

universe and his or her relation with the world—including the world of action, ethics, and history—and not only the validity of the science we possess.

In this context, two opposed and complementary directions are to be observed. On the one hand, Kant's revolution places the human subject at the metaphysical/philosophical center, as a constitutive and determining factor with respect to the world and within it.[2] On the other hand, human reason, in all its doings, is inexorably dependent on the presence of sensible material—the given of Being—without which the spontaneous activity of reason could not take place, or would be meaningless and void of content. As a result, Kant distinguishes himself from all his predecessors who were philosophers of reason—from Plato to Descartes and from Spinoza to Leibniz and from the thinkers of the pre-Critical enlightenment—and stands in dual opposition to them: first, in ascribing to human reason an extraordinary power within its legitimate domain, and second, in radically shrinking and limiting this domain. Hence, as much as Kant is the modern philosopher of reason in its world-shaping role, he is also the genuine philosopher of reason's *finitude* and the finitude of the human being.

The Critique as Self-Consciousness and as an Act of Autonomy

This duality already inheres in the Kantian concept of critique, which has an affirmative and a negative side. The Critique is a complex reflective act in which philosophical reason explores and examines *itself*. Due to his tendency to legal metaphors, Kant assigns the Critique the mission "to institute a court of justice, by which reason may secure its rightful claims while dismissing all its groundless pretensions, and this not by mere

---

2. Copernicus dwarfed man's *physical* place in the universe, while Kant responds with upgrading man's *metaphysical* role.

decrees but according to its own eternal and unchangeable laws."[3] The ruling of this court is based upon a descriptive examination of the facts and functions of reason that allows to determine its limits and pass judgment on all its claims, the valid and the invalid. In this respect, the Critique is first of all a mode of philosophical self-consciousness. Kant argues that such self-consciousness must precede and prepare, and also criticize in advance, all claims to know objects. The knowing human subject must first know itself, its mental capabilities and inexorable ontological limitations, before trying to determine anything about the world, what it contains, and what is supposed to lie beyond it.

In calling his Critique "an essay on method" Kant links onto an issue that has been on the philosophical agenda since Bacon and Descartes. Most premodern philosophers (excepting Spinoza) agreed that prior to setting out to know, one must study and determine the nature of knowledge itself and how it is legitimately obtained.[4] Kant widely broadens this approach: in order to know the ways and modes of knowledge one must first know the *knowing being*, and the spectrum of his or her capabilities— mainly, though not only, the a priori capabilities, those that are not derived from experience. The Critique, says Kant, in performing this task, serves as "propaedeutic" (preparatory essay) to a new, valid metaphysics that would at long last count as a rigorous science rather than mere opinion. However, we should notice that the Critique itself already supplies substantive philosophical contents and not merely a formal method, and can therefore be seen as a *philosophical science of self-consciousness*

3. *Critique of Pure Reason*, trans. and ed. Paul Guyer and Allen W. Wood (Cambridge: Cambridge University Press, 1998), preface of the first edition (Axi–xii).

4. Spinoza claimed, against the mainstream of modern philosophy, that in order to know what certain knowledge is, one should already possess certain knowledge. Therefore, substantive knowledge is prior to knowing the method, and is even a precondition for it.

and a kind of "metaphysics of metaphysics," as Kant himself once called it.[5]

This new metaphysics that the Critique was to prepare was meant to branch off into two branches, a critical metaphysics of *nature* (including epistemology and ontology), and a critical metaphysics of *moral action* (including law, politics, history, and a moral religion). But again, it turns out that the Critique itself offers a substantive theory, not only of self-consciousness but also of the foundations of the natural world. For, according to the "Copernican" principle set by the Critique, the conditions for *thinking* objects in nature are equally the conditions for these *to be* objects in nature. Therefore, in knowing the grounds of thinking natural objects we at once know the first grounds of nature itself, that is, we possess what Kant calls "a pure science of nature" (and also, "nature in a formal sense"). Based on these foundations and on sensible materials, we also need an *empirical* science of nature (such as physics and its derivatives in astronomy, organic chemistry, biology), since it is only by empirical science that we come to know particular objects and specific natural laws, and even to know there is a world. And since empirical science is based on the a priori science, we are able to know in advance, as a conditional proposition, that *if* there is a natural world and there are natural objects in it, they all necessarily obey certain primary conditions, which the Critique determines and formulates a priori. In this respect, the Critique that exhibits the science of consciousness generates, by the same move, an a priori science of the foundations of nature.

This is the affirmative aspect of the Critique: discovering the legitimate power of the understanding in constituting the formal foundations of nature. Yet the same reason that affirms this power and ascribes it to itself at the same time realizes its boundaries and forbids itself to contravene them. This is its negative role. In Kant's legal metaphor, reason stands trial before its own court:

---

5. In a letter to Marcus Hertz, 11 May 1781.

not only does it discover its limits through a *cognitive* act, it also determines itself, in an act of will, to respect those limits and prevail over the temptation to transgress them, a temptation that Kant sees as inherent in the nature of rationality and therefore as possessing a privileged power, which nevertheless must and can be overcome. This means, in Kantian terms, that *the Critique performs an act of autonomy already in the field of knowledge.*

Kant's concept of autonomy is usually associated with the areas of action and morality, where it refers to the will that restrains itself according to the laws of its own rational nature (as spelled out in the categorical imperative) and thereby attains self-determination and freedom. A similar pattern exists (latently) in the critique of knowledge: theoretical reason restrains itself—not in an arbitrary and accidental way but "according to the eternal and unchangeable" laws of reason itself (see the quote above, Axii), and thus realizes itself and becomes autonomous. In less doctrinal words, by submitting to the limits of reason, with all the pain and sense of loss this may entail, there lies a constructive liberating force.

Finite Rational Beings

Accordingly, Kant calls the human being "a limited rational being" and also "a finite thinking being." Both adjectives, "rational" and "finite," are equally essential to the definition (and to each other). The human being is not rational in separation from his finitude; rather, his reason is finite and his finitude rational. This intermediation is central to Kant's theory of man. We cannot be rational except through reason's finitude, just as this finitude must be attributed to us as creatures of reason from the outset.

No Intellectual Intuition

A major expression of human finitude is the ontological fact that we have no intellectual intuition nor an intuiting intellect. By intuition Kant understands the perception of particulars, and by intellectual activity he means the thinking of universal concepts and principles. An intuiting intellect (an imaginary construct) would, by thinking a universal concept or principle, know immediately all the particulars that fall within the range of that universal principle, without having to acquire them inductively from external sources, like sense perception. And intellectual intuition is one that observes a single particular and immediately sees in it the full power of the corresponding universal, without the need to go through all other particulars in order to draw the universal from them. These two modes of perception express one and a single capability, by whose negation the human finitude is defined, namely, the power to grasp immediately, without further assistance, the universal factor within a single particular and the totality of particulars within the common universal they share. The activity of such an intellect is creative throughout, devoid of all sensibility and subject to no external influence, yet particularizes itself into specific contents.

Kant does not say there are actually creatures with such superhuman qualities, nor that there is a God who fulfills this ideal; he uses this superhuman image only as a model against which to define our own limitations, the kind of rationality we *do not* possess. The starting point of the Critique is that *humans are not endowed with an intuitive intellect.* Our intellect can only think, and our intuition can only perceive particulars. In other words, human intellect is discursive and not intuitive,[6] and human intuition is always sensible and never intellectual. These two, thinking and intuition (more precisely, sensation, which serves intuition as material), are two radically distinct operations that should by no means be confused. Rather, their rigorous separation is the living nerve of the Critique. The intellect's action is spontaneous and flows from itself, whereas

---

6. Intuitive—grasping immediately or seeing at once the entirety of the issue; discursive—gaining knowledge by the mediation of universal concepts, deductions, and inferences, etc.

sensation is receptive, and passively driven by outside stimuli (just as the British empiricists described it). Thereby the intellect is considered pure and a priori, contrary to sensation, which is empirical and a posteriori. Yet the intellect is merely formal, and depends on sense perception in order to receive the necessary data for the cognition of objects. Therefore, albeit the fundamental heterogeneity between them, our intuition and understanding must work together in order for us to have an objective cognition and an empirical world to be cognized. Here it is worthwhile quoting Kant's own words:

> Our cognition arises from two fundamental sources in the mind, the first of which is the reception of representations (the receptivity of impressions), the second the faculty for cognizing an object by means of these representations (spontaneity of concepts); through the former an object is *given* to us, through the latter it is *thought* in relation to that representation (as a mere determination of the mind). Intuitions and concepts therefore constitute the elements of all our cognitions, so that neither concepts without intuitions corresponding to them in some way nor intuition without concepts can yield a cognition. Both are either pure or empirical. *Empirical*, if sensation (which presupposes the actual presence of the object) is contained therein; but *pure* if no sensation is mixed into the representation. (A50/B74)

> If we will call the *receptivity* of our mind to receive representations insofar as it is affected in some way *sensibility*, then on the contrary the faculty bringing forth representations itself, or the *spontaneity* of cognitions, is the *understanding*. It comes along with our nature that *intuition* can never be other than *sensible*, i.e. that it contains only the way in which we are affected by objects. The faculty for *thinking* of objects of sensible intuition, on the contrary, is the *understanding*. Neither of these properties is to be preferred to the other. Without sensibility no object would be given to us, and

without understanding none would be thought. Thoughts without content are empty, intuitions without concepts are blind. . . . These two faculties or capacities cannot exchange their functions. The understanding is not capable of intuiting anything and the senses are not capable of thinking anything. Only from their unification can cognition arise. But on this account one must not mix up their roles, rather one has great cause to separate them carefully from each other and distinguish them. (A51–52/B75–76)

The radical heterogeneity between these two sources— spontaneity and receptivity, or the pure and the sensible—is the foundation of the rigorous dualism that characterizes Kant in *all* parts of his system. Kant needs to sharply separate between the two in order to maintain critical purity in knowledge and in ethics, yet on the other hand he needs to link them reciprocally to ensure the possibility of knowing objects and performing moral action. Hence the problem of bridging the duality (known as "schematism" in the broad sense) that recurs in most parts of his system: what is it that enables the two poles to come together despite their stark heterogeneity? Some Kant followers suggested that both the intellect and the senses branch off from a secret and unknowable common root, but Kant adamantly rejected this solution. The unknowable source can only be intellectual intuition, and whoever affirms the existence of such a source is already claiming to know and to use it. The question of the common source lies beyond the scope of reason, and the Critique, which expresses the structure of the rational creature we are, must necessarily start from human duality as an unshakable fact.

Skepticism and Dogmatism

The Critique also traces Kant's road between the two great ills he finds in philosophy, dogmatism and skepticism. Dogmatism ascribes to human reason capacities it does not possess, and skepticism denies it the capabilities it does possess. The first builds groundless castles in the air, the second undermines all the grounded buildings. Thus dogmatism is flawed by excessive affirmation and skepticism by excessive negation, whereas the Critique, after rigorous scrutiny, combines within itself the negation and affirmation in a state of reciprocal and balanced tension. Historically, Kant associates dogmatism with Leibniz's rationalist school and skepticism with the British empiricists; at the same time he finds that each of those opposing movements also commits its opponent's fallacy: empiricist skepticism is dogmatic since it does not question its own presuppositions, and rationalist dogmatism breeds skepticism because it leads to inner contradictions in reason.

Dogmatism is usually understood as a stubborn or habitual attachment to an unproven position. Kant gives the concept further, more specific interpretations. First, Kant's dogmatist is a philosopher of reason who not only affirms something without proof, but also fails to check whether *in principle* it can be proved (or refuted). Second, the term "dogmatism" indicates in Kant not only a flawed intellectual disposition, but also a specific philosophical position, the one his Copernican revolution is out to reverse. A dogmatic in Kant's vocabulary takes it for granted that objects are things in themselves, and that reason can derive existence from mere concepts without the cooperation of experience. The dogmatic therefore believes that reason can know what lies beyond experience, to penetrate into the "interior" of things, as it were, and rise to the knowledge of God, the freedom of the will, immortality, and the cosmos as totality—the traditional queries of metaphysics.

Among the dogmatists Kant counts all the rationalists since antiquity, including Plato, Aristotle, the scholastics of the late Middle Ages and the Renaissance, and in recent generations— Leibniz, with his army of followers, and he himself, Kant, in his precritical period. In those years, Kant says, he had been submerged in "dogmatic slumber," until skeptical challenges drove him to discover a new road. Who exactly awoke Kant from his slumber? Kant's answer has two versions. In a famous place in the *Prolegomena* Kant gives the credit to Hume,[7] while elsewhere he attributes his awakening to the antinomy of reason.[8] These two sources are allegedly distinct, but as we shall see later, they are actually linked.

By the antinomy of reason Kant refers to the contradictions that inhere in philosophical reasoning when it tries to conceive of the world in its totality and describe its characteristics without critique. Does the world in itself have a beginning in time? Is it finite or infinite in space? Is the world made up of free, contingent events, or is it deterministic? Questions such as these have resulted in paradoxes and contradictions ever since Zeno of Elea—especially when the answer takes on the form of formal proof. Thus the authority of reason was undermined as contradictory arguments were equally supported by reason.

Kant started with the presupposition he held unshakable, that reason, by its very concept, cannot contradict itself. Therefore, if nevertheless we encounter a stubborn antinomy that refuses to disappear, it must necessarily be a merely apparent contradiction that, however, is deeply rooted in our ordinary ways of thinking. From here Kant's way led to searching for the deep causes of the contradiction, and their removal. The conclusion of this investigation was that seeming contradictions occur when our mode of thinking takes the objects of our knowledge to be things in themselves. Therefore the Copernican reversal is needed, which replaces the dogmatic way of thinking with a critical way that sharply distinguishes between objects as phenomena and as things in themselves. Thereby naïve realism is replaced by the philosophical outlook Kant names Transcendental Idealism. And since the latter allows, as

---

7. *Prolegomena to Any Future Metaphysics*, trans. L. W. Beck (Indianapolis: Bobbs-Merrill, 1950), introduction, 8.

8. A407/B434, and regarding the cosmological idea, *Prolegomena* §50.

by-product, to solve the antinomy and restore reason to itself as a coherent system, Kant sees this result as reinforcing the reversal he suggested.

David Hume, as Kant reads him, actually awoke Kant twice: first, as a modern skeptic who destroys the possibility of the new science, and consequently also as a classical skeptic who finds contractions and *aporias* in reason. Hume had started from Locke's empiricist doctrine, which states that all our valid concepts, and even the Understanding (intellect) itself, are derived exclusively from experience. From here Hume rightly concluded that on this basis we shall never be able to reach an objective being, nor universal and necessary natural laws and phenomena. Our natural laws will always rely on incomplete induction and therefore will never be truly universal, and our ideas will be linked by merely accidental associations that do not necessarily express an objective reality. Conclusion: from the philosophical standpoint, a universal and necessary science is impossible. On the other side, Kant could not imagine Hume denying Newton's laws nor their mathematical demonstrations or foundations. On the contrary, he assumed that Hume's "good sense" would force him to accept the mathematical physics of his time even though his rational-philosophical reasoning tells him—necessarily, given his empiricist assumptions—that such a science is impossible. Result: a valid natural science is both real and impossible—a contradiction that undermines the very authority of reason.[9]

The cause of this contradiction, Kant thought, was not the failure of empirical natural science as such, but the failure of philosophical reason, *as long as it is based on empiricist assumptions.* Hence, in order to explain the possibility of natural science we must abandon the assumptions of empiricism and assume instead that the understanding is an independent and

9. According to my interpretation, this is how Kant understood Hume. (I do not necessarily imply it is how Hume himself meant to be understood.)

separate a priori fact, and that it is the action of the pure understanding that introduces the necessary connections into the matter of experience, thus constituting an object and an objective world.[10]

From here one can see that Kant's struggle against skepticism and dogmatism concerns not only method but content as well. It does not simply seek a middle position between the two but anticipates Kant's distinctive positive philosophy. The same Copernican thesis that replaces dogmatism is also meant to refute the skeptics in both their ancient rationalist form and their modern empiricist version, and its success in doing so provides a reinforcement of the revolutionary thesis.[11]

The term "reason" has several meanings in Kant. Its broadest sense refers to the human mind in its general capacity for intellectual thinking and self-consciousness—that which distinguishes us as humans. In a much narrower sense, the term points to all the mind's *pure* (absolutely a priori) functions, those that contain no sensible elements and are not derived from the senses. (As we shall see later, there is also pure intuition and pure imagination in Kant, and not only pure thinking.) Finally, pure thinking works either as "understanding" (*Verstand*) or as "reason" (*Vernunft*) in a restricted technical sense. Understanding/ *Verstand* works by applying itself to the senses, while reason/ *Vernunft* does not relate to the senses, but works to systematically order the scientific products of the intellect, while striving, beyond them, to take off toward an unconditioned reality.

The title "critique of pure reason" connotes all three. (1) The Critique explores and maps the overall range of human

10. It is worth noting that Hume himself mentions such a conclusion, but dismisses it as an absurd idea that contradicts common sense. Kant, however, dared taking this allegedly absurd idea seriously, and used it as a foundation for a new worldview.

11. The indirect confirmation of the Copernican turn will be addressed in detail when we discuss the "regressive argument" of the Transcendental Deduction and the antinomies.

intellectual capacity; (2) it concentrates especially on the mind's "pure" or a priori functions; (3) the Critique's negative and re-straining side refers to reason in the transcendent narrow sense, that is, dogmatic rational theology and philosophy that claims to know the unknowable.

Actually there is in Kant no notion of reason as such, as a Pla-tonic idea; there are *creatures* of reason, for whom finite ratio-nality is their essential mode of being and acting. Kant insists he is investigating this activity not as a causal process in time, that is, not as an empirical psychologist would study them, but as a philosopher investigating the atemporal forms by which objects are thought. Thus he sets up a new kind of logic (a "'transcen-dental logic") supplanting the formal logic (see later). Kant was interested in deciphering these forms of logic (in knowledge and ethics) so that some readers get the impression that reason for him was an inert formal calculus, a system of mere static rules. However, Kantian reason, by its nature and source, is always the activity of a rational *subject* operating in the first person and capable (at least latently) to say "I" to itself in all its thoughts, perceptions, feelings, and acts of will.

Furthermore, the subject-dependent Kantian reason is not inert. It is driven by certain inner tendencies that strive toward goals that inhere in rationality itself. Therefore, to get a fuller view of Kant's background assumptions, we should consider his concept of "the interests of reason."

The Interests of Reason and Its History

The "interests of reason" is a key concept in Kant's meta-philosophy and, in different variations, recurs hundreds of times in his works. In the Critique it is implied in the two prefaces and arises again, more explicitly, toward the end, in the chap-ters on the *architectonic of reason* and the *history of reason*. From these meta-philosophical texts it is clear that the history of reason—its self-discovery and self-explication throughout the

ages—depends according to Kant on the clash between opposite
interests of reason and the attempts to reconcile them.[12]

By reason's "architectonic" Kant means the art of building a
system by which a cluster of random cognitions is given a scientific coherence and quasi-organic unity (see A832/B860). Kant
emphasizes that the unification of the many ingredients into a
system depends on the *goal* or *end* that organizes it. If the goals
are external or accidental from reason's viewpoint, the unity of
the system is merely *technical*.[13] A truly architectonic unity is
achieved only when the organizing end of a system expresses
the *essential ends* of reason. As human reason is limited and
borne by a finite subject, the essential ends of reason are not
necessarily in a state of realization; rather, reason strives to realize the ends imprinted in it, and this striving is configured as an
interest of reason. In different contexts (historical, cultural, political, philosophical) it may well be that different rational interests look contradictory or actually clash; yet this cannot be their
fundamental state. Hence the task of creating a valid philosophy
requires us to reconcile different rational interests and find the
right architectonic balance between them. The continued effort
to do this is the history of reason—embodied in the history of
philosophy—in which reason partially explicates itself to itself,
while also generating obscurity and contradictions.

The nuclear paradigm of the system of reason is latent in
human reason from its infancy, and comes into partial and
flawed view in the various historical systems of philosophy. Philosophical progress may be achieved piecemeal on some dispa-
rate particular issues, but the systems built upon them, being
one-sided and contradictory, must eventually collapse, leaving
their ruins as building blocks for a later philosopher to pick up

12. Different versions of this necessary and dynamic link between rationality
and subjectivity are characteristic of German Idealism.

13. In these cases reason acts instrumentally, serving not its own ends but
the interests of others (as do strategists and technological systems).

for his new construction—which must expect a similar fate; and this process continues as long as the critique of reason has not performed its revolution.

Thus Kant identifies in the philosophical culture of his time a clash between the metaphysical interest of reason, embodied in Leibniz's dogmatic rationalism, and its critical interest, expressed one-sidedly in Hume's skepticism. The history of reason is thus the historization of its pure paradigm, the actual shape that reason's interests have assumed in their partial, one-sided, and contradictory embodiments in past philosophical trends and masters.[14]

Kant writes:

> Systems seem to have been formed, like maggots, by a *generatio aequivoca*, from the mere confluence of aggregated concepts, garbled at first but complete in time, although they all had their schema, as the original seed, in the mere self-development of reason, and on that account are not merely each articulated for themselves in accordance with an idea but are rather all in turn purposively united with each other as members of a whole in a system of human cognition, and allow an architectonic to all human knowledge, which at the present time, since so much material has already been collected or can be taken from the ruins of collapsed older edifices, would not merely be possible but would not even be very difficult. (A835/B863)

This historical process is driven by the interests of reason. Reason's interests are inherent to it and not directed to any external goal. In other words, *human rationality is a goal-oriented activity, whose goal lies in itself rather than in anything other than itself.* The common interest (call it a meta-interest) is the

---

14. It is surprising to notice how, in this argument, Kant anticipates ideas that were later ascribed to Hegel.

realization of rationality as end in itself in the various domains of human activity: in knowledge, in the activity of the will (morality, social, and political life), and also in the areas of beauty and the sublime. The striving for rationality thus takes different modes that constitute special interests of reason, including the *theoretical* interest (to know the world), the *practical* interest (to morally reshape the world), and also the *aesthetic* interest.[15] In addition there are rational interests that work in all domains: the *metaphysical* interest of reason, its *critical* interest, and the *architectonic* interest that seeks to establish the right balance between the other interests and to resolve the oppositions that occur between them in a given philosophical culture.

The topic of "The History of Pure Reason" (the last section in the book) was left undeveloped by Kant. But other, scattered, pages allow the following reconstruction of his views.

The metaphysical interest had characterized reason since ancient times and has gone through several transformations. This is the drive toward the absolute, the supersensible, the infinite, and the total. One cannot abolish this interest without abolishing rationality itself. Rationality demands a sufficient reason for everything finite, and will not cease until its explanations cover everything. Hence, the drive to transcend the world of finitude and the senses and rise to the infinite and total is essential to the human mind, and it would be irrational to disregard or try to eliminate it. However this drive has time and again generated fallacies and delusions, from ancient magic and mythology to religion in its several variations, and again to theology and the systems of dogmatic metaphysics that arose throughout the

---

15. The aesthetic interest is directed to the experiences of beauty as a universally valid judgment, and of sublimity as the embodiment of the infinite. Moreover, like cognitive truth and like the moral will, the beautiful is free from external interests, and its end is nothing but itself. These characteristics suggest that the beautiful embodies the essential features of Kantian rationality.

ages. In all of these, a genuine rational interest was given a false and distorted expression.

Unlike the primeval metaphysical interest, the critical interest is basically modern. In fact, its rise characterizes modernity. In its wider scope this interest demands to reexamine accepted beliefs and entrenched ways of thought and practice; but in a narrower sense it forbids making claims about real existence where no relevant sense perception is given—or *can* be given. Among other things, this means that any attempt to infer the existence of things from mere concepts, which is the way of thinking of the scholastics and of traditional ontology or metaphysics generally, is strictly banned.[16] Finally, reason's architectonic interest seeks to overcome the tensions and oppositions between its specific interests (the result of their being falsely interpreted), and to reconfigure them according to their true meaning, so that they complement each other in one coherent system.

Kant described his project in three programmatic texts: the two prefaces to the *Critique of Pure Reason* and the opening sections of the *Prolegomena*, and in all three he says it responds to the urgent need to resolve the antinomy that arose in reason between the metaphysical interest and the critical interest. Both are necessary conditions of rationality, yet they oppose each other in the contemporary philosophical culture. While many cling obstinately to an antiquated, "worm-eaten" metaphysics, others despise all metaphysics or treat it with indifference. Kant diagnoses this indifference as feigned and built on self-deception. "It is pointless to affect **indifference** with respect to such inquiries, to whose object human nature **cannot be indifferent**" (Ax). Nevertheless, Kant realizes that the indifference does not express lightweight thinking, but results from the "ripened **power of judgment [of the age]**, which will no longer be

16. We already saw that Kant has a specific concept of "dogmatism"; parallel to it, he has a specific sense of "critique." Both concern the claim to derive reality from an a priori concept (without the aid of intuition).

put off with illusory knowledge" (Axi). This power is the critical drive of reason that attained maturity in the age of Enlightenment, and now has the task of creating the basis for a new, critical metaphysics, which would reconcile the different interests of reason and have the status of "science," that is, a valid and certain body of knowledge.[17] This, he says, is his goal not only in the present Critique but also in those to follow, suggesting that practical philosophy will also belong to the critical metaphysics, and serve as a metaphysics of morals.

17. With these explicit declarations, Kant disproves a long tradition of interpretation that was especially current in the English-speaking world, according to which Kant had destroyed metaphysics. Kant, however, believed that he only abolished the possibility for dogmatic metaphysics, and established the critical metaphysics in its place. In the following pages we will see how he could justify this view.

PART TWO

Following Kant's Argument

THE ABOVE PAGES looked at the *Critique* from a more general perspective. (Textually, they also covered the book's two prefaces.) The rest of this book—its main body—presents a brief account of the work's main topics and arguments in the order of its chapters. The textual basis is edition B, with a few complements from A.

The Introduction

Kant's introduction (written for edition A and extended in B) contains some of the main concepts and claims that stand at the book's background all along. These include his definitions of a priori and a posteriori; the distinction between analytic and synthetic judgments; the claim that mathematical propositions are synthetic; and the reformulation of his task—to create a critical metaphysics—in terms of the question about the possibility of synthetic a priori judgments.

A Priori and A Posteriori. These terms served in the scholastic literature to indicate that which comes before and that which comes after. Kant uses them in a meaning of his own, in which the "before" and the "after" refer to experience. An a priori concept or content is neither derived from experience nor

dependent on it; in this sense it is "before" experience or precedes it. On the other hand an a posteriori concept or content is
possible only on the basis of some sensible experience (inner or
outer) and is derived from it. Hence, an a priori concept or proposition can be known as true prior to any experience, whereas an
a posteriori proposition depends on experience as a condition
for being known and verified.

Kant emphasizes that his philosophy deals with the absolutely a priori, not the relative one. A relative a priori is exempli-
fied in a sentence like "the man could have known a priori that
the balloon will explode if placed near the fire." The man's possible prior knowledge is derived from experience and as such is
essentially a posteriori and empirical. Kant's concern is with an
a priori that has no origin in experience whatsoever. He calls this
absolute a priori "pure" in contrast to "empirical."

Transcendental and Transcendent. The distinction between
a priori and a posteriori stands at the background of Kant's special concept of the transcendental. Here again Kant borrowed
a scholastic concept and fitted it to his needs.[1] Not only does a
(valid) transcendental element not depend on experience, but
experience itself depends on it and is made possible by it. As we
are to see later, such are the pure categories of the understanding, which make the world of experience possible. Every transcendental element is also a priori, but not vice versa: our understanding and discourse contain many a priori elements that are
not transcendental, because the possibility of experience does
not depend on them; for example, all the judgments Kant calls
analytic.

We should also distinguish between transcenden*tal* and
transcen*dent.* Although this distinction is crucial to Kant, he
is not always scrupulous in observing it (and the line between
the two concepts has become blurred in their English-language

---

1. The definition of this concept is not included in the introduction, but has
relevance to this issue.

use). A *transcendental* element (a concept, a principle) has the following features: (a) it is not derived from experience; (b) the possibility of experience depends on it; (c) it has no meaning and no valid use except in application to the world of experience. Such elements are the foundations of Kant's critical metaphysics and the pillars of the objective world as he conceives it. On the other hand, a *transcendent* element shares only in the first feature. It is not derived from experience, and is also inapplicable to experience. Hence it is not restrained and controlled by sensation and observation, but breaks the boundaries of the empirical world altogether, which renders it empty and invalid. This is the domain of illusory metaphysics that serves as principal target of the Critique's negative function.

Analytic and Synthetic Judgments. Leibniz distinguished between eternal (timeless) truths, which are necessary by their meaning alone and cannot therefore be negated without contradiction, and factual truths, which are logically contingent and could also have been different. Hume, too, suggested a similar duality—between necessary relations and matters of fact. Kant joins together these insights in the famous distinction, which has become associated with his name, between analytic and synthetic judgments. A judgment is a unit of discourse that combines a subject and a predicate.[2] When the concept of the predicate is contained (implied) in the concept of the subject, and can be derived from it by mere logical analysis without additional information, the judgment is analytic. For example, "the building occupies a place in space" or "my uncle is a relative of mine." In such judgments we need not go beyond the information contained in the subject; we merely explicate what it implies. Basically an analytic judgment is tautological, because its predicate only repeats what is implicitly said in the subject and

---

2. Kant alternates between the terms "judgment" (*Urteil*) and "proposition" (*Satz*), but "judgment" is the more accurate and better suited to his teaching (as will be seen in the deduction of the categories).

makes it explicit. But sometimes the implication is so veiled and indirect, that one needs a rather complex analysis to bring it to light. Therefore analytic judgments have often a significant role in the process of knowledge, although they do not expand it.

An analytic judgment is always a priori and necessary, since its truth derives from its very meaning. Its test, says Kant, is the law of noncontradiction; that is, when negating the judgment generates a self-contradiction, the judgment is analytic. (The sentence "my uncle is not my relative" actually says, "my relative is not my relative," and the sentence "the building does not occupy a place in space" actually says, "a thing that occupies a place in space does not occupy a place in space.")

On the other hand, in a synthetic judgment the concept of the predicate goes beyond the concept of the subject and adds more information to it. For example, "the building occupies a place on Broadway" or "my uncle is a relative of the mayor." The additional information differs from everything contained in the subject and no analysis or dismantling can lead to it. Therefore the negation of a synthetic judgment will not generate a contradiction, although it can be *false*. In other words, a synthetic judgment can be either true or false, but its falsity will be due to its failure to correspond to the state of affairs to which it points, and not self-contradiction.

Typical examples of synthetic judgments that extend knowledge are those drawn from experience. Such judgments are a posteriori by definition, and the connection they set between subject and predicate lacks necessity, whereas analytic propositions are a priori, and the connection they establish between subject and predicate is a necessary one. If we arrange the two distinctions—a priori/a posteriori and analytic/synthetic—we get the relationships shown in Table 1.

Box 1 is necessarily empty since all analytic judgments are a priori. This is precisely the reason why box 2 is not empty: it contains all possible analytic judgments. Box 3 also has many members, namely, all the judgments derived from experience.

Table 1. A Matrix of Basic Relations

	A Posteriori	A Priori
Analytic	(1) −	(2) +
Synthetic	(3) +	(4) ?

So far the table would be acceptable also to the empiricist philosophers. The dividing question that separates them from Kant lies in box 4. Here are supposed to exist synthetic judgments that are not derived from experience, and yet establish a *nonanalytic* connection between two contents, neither of which is implied in the other. Are such synthetic a priori judgments possible, and if so—this is the important question to Kant—what *makes them possible*?

Locke and Hume argue that box 4 is empty. Kant claims that the evolution of the exact sciences demonstrates, on the contrary, that synthetic a priori elements do operate in the sciences, and it is they that endow mathematics and physics with the property of universality and necessity, which they undeniably possess, yet which cannot be derived from experience. If we can offer a theory that explains how these elements are possible—by investigating their origin, scope, and uses—we shall upgrade metaphysics, too, to the state of science.

Mathematical Propositions Are All Synthetic. Contrary to the prevailing view, Kant argues that mathematical propositions are not only a priori but also synthetic. This is because the concepts used in geometry and arithmetic are the products of a special mental function he calls "pure intuition." By intuition in general Kant understands the perception of particular individuals: empirical intuition perceives individuals by sensation, that is, a posteriori, while pure intuition perceives its proper objects a priori. Pure intuition is neither sensation nor conceptual thought, but a mental function in its own kind (sui generis) which, like sensation, is related to particulars yet has the universal force of conceptual thinking. Pure intuition works by perceiving a priori a basic singular unit—in geometry it is a unit of space, in arithmetic the number—and transcends it toward other units of the same kind existing outside it. This creates a homogeneous continuum, from which the basic mathematical entities—lines, spatial figures, and numeric values—are constructed. The act that links the basic unit to others like it (or rather, to itself) involves each time a new synthesis that adds to the series a member that wasn't there before, and cannot be deduced from its predecessors by analysis. The novelty here lies not in the content of the new member but in the new intuiting *act* that is required to produce it.

Kant does not claim that such a process occurs each time we perform a mathematical operation, but that it stands at the origin of the mathematical *concepts and entities* that serve us in mathematics. The number 5 is the product of a construction that adds the basic numerical unit to itself and stops at the fifth place. Therefore we cannot deduce the number but must construct it with the help of intuition in the way described. In the proposition 7 + 5 = 12 the number 12 is not contained conceptually either in 5 or in 7, and also not in the sign "+" that connects them. Kant says: "no matter how long I analyze my concept of such a possible sum I will still not find twelve in it" (B15). I reach the 12 by adding the basic unit to itself until the number 5, and then go on to extend the continuum with seven more places. (The formula 5 + 7 = 12 represents in this way the building instruction of the magnitude in question.)[3] Similarly, spatial formations like points, lines, and volumes are the product of synthetic construction in space. Thus the mathematical sciences have a synthetic character due to the need for a new synthesis at any additional stage of constructing a number

---

3. Kant does not say that we perform this entire process in everyday life; we have learned to rely on our memory and certain automatic rules of manipulating numbers, which already *use* constructed numbers but do not reflect their genesis.

or a geometrical figure, and because in this process, "help must be gotten from intuition, by means of which alone the synthesis is possible" (B16).

This famous (and much contested) view belongs to Kant's broader view of mathematics, in which the pure imagination with its work of "construction in time" plays a central role.[4]

So far Kant has identified one area in which a priori and synthetic elements are at work—pure mathematics. While this science does not yet investigate the empirical world, but only the formal relations in the realm of numbers and figures, physics and the other empirical sciences apply the laws of pure mathematics to the processes of the real world, and use them to deduce and foresee real processes and events in nature. The role of the Critique will be to explain (a) what enables the validity of mathematical principles in themselves (this is discussed in the Transcendental Aesthetics) and (b) what enables them, as applied mathematics ("the mathematics of phenomena") to dictate their laws to real objects in nature (this is discussed in "The Analytic of Transcendental Principles: The 'Pure Science of Nature'").

In addition to mathematics, Kant identifies the work of synthetic a priori propositions also in the natural sciences, starting with physics. The scientific revolution of the seventeenth century as embodied in Newton's physics was received as an apodictic science no less than Euclidean geometry; and although an empirical science, it is informed and determined by a cluster of a priori elements without which such a science would not have been possible. Kant cites as examples the principles of inertia, of the preservation of matter, and of the equality of action and reaction. These principles, alongside the principle of causality, are to be discussed as part of "The Analytic of Transcendental Principles:

---

4. In the twentieth century attempts were made to refute Kant's intuitionism regarding mathematics by actually deriving the foundations of mathematics from logic—the best known attempt is Bertrand Russell and A. N. Whitehead's *Principia Mathematica*—but the debate is still alive.

The 'Pure Science of Nature'"; together they constitute according to Kant a pure physics that is embedded in empirical physics and "deserves to be separately established, as a science of its own, in its whole domain, whether narrow or wide" (B21 note).[5]

This is the ground that allowed Kant to reformulate the question of metaphysics-as-science in terms of the question of synthetic a priori judgments. The reformulation was introduced in the *Prolegomena* (1783) and in edition B of the Critique (1787), in order to sharpen the focus of the problem before him, but should not be understood as narrowing the wider philosophical perspective presented above.

On the Structure of the Book

The formal structure of the Critique recalls the familiar divisions of books on logic and philosophy in the German academy of his time. The main division is between a *doctrine of elements* and a *doctrine of method*; the first, despite its title, holds the main body of the critical system, while the second supplements it with related meta-philosophical discussions. The doctrine of elements is divided into a Transcendental Aesthetics (theory of sensation) and a Transcendental Logic (conceptual thinking). The latter divides into a transcendental analytic and a transcendental dialectic. The transcendental analytic contains the valid, experience-oriented part of the critical metaphysics, while the Dialectic (the logic of illusion) contains its false and misleading part. Yet the Dialectic has one important positive function: it turns the metaphysical interest, which aims at transcending experience, into a regulative idea that endows the metaphysical interest with an immanent, critical use in the empirical world. The

---

5. The reservation is due to the fact that this science—which Kant sometimes calls the "pure natural science"—is indeed limited in scope. Moreover, it is divided into an original level and derived level; and the Critique deals only with the former.

Analytic is further divided into the analytic of *Concepts*, with the theory of categories at its center, and the analytic of *Principles*, revolving around the synthetic a priori principles that rely on the categories and constitute the "pure science of nature."

It is interesting to note that Kant's mode of writing is fast and succinct at first, and slows down as he goes on; so the volume of text devoted to each topic expands as the book progresses. This is a well-known phenomenon in many writers. Of course, the length of the chapters is not a gauge of their systematic importance to Kant. The Transcendental Aesthetics, to which we now turn, is probably the most succinct in the book, yet Kant considers it crucial both in itself and to all that follows.

Space and Time as Forms of Intuition: The Transcendental Aesthetics

By "Transcendental Aesthetics" Kant means a doctrine concerning the synthetic a priori elements of intuition.[6] This is apparently a paradox: our intuition (the perception of particulars) derives from the senses, and the senses are supposed to be passive and primary, that is, to perceive simple, immediate data, which nothing precedes or mediates. This is not only the view of the empiricists; many philosophers, including Descartes and his followers, as well as modern positivists, talk about an immediate sensible perception that provides simple impressions as building blocks for complex concepts. Kant, throughout the Critique, combats against the notion of simplicity, not only in conceptual thinking and the consciousness of the "I think," but already on the level of sense perception.

---

6. Aesthetics in this sense is not knowledge about beauty, but the cognitive science of intuition. Intuition, in the Kantian sense, is the apprehension of particulars by one of the senses, which can be external (sight, touch, etc.) or internal. The inner sense is the perception of inner mental events (which empiricism called "reflection").

The first radical move made by the Critique is the claim that intuition is not merely passive, and that sense perception alone, by itself, is unable to supply particular data. Passive sensation is not yet intuition: it is nothing but shapeless, indefinite material that requires certain forms of order and organization *already for the sake of sense perception itself,* and for our ability to distinguish separate individuals in it. These patterns of order are provided by the mind to itself by means of the a priori forms of space and of time.

Accordingly, the act of intuition is divided into matter and form. The matter of intuition is sensation in its diverse variety, while the form of intuition is the sensation's location and interrelations within the frames of time and space. The object of intuition—the sensible phenomenon—is always subject to the minimal order determined by time and space. Moreover, these forms of intuition—time and space—make possible the individuation of the sensible impressions, due to which the sensations are separate from each other (in Kant's idiom: "outside one another") and appear to be simple. Actually, their simplicity is imaginary. They are indeed singular items, but this is already the *result* of being arranged in the pattern of "one by the other" (space) and "one after the other" (time), or more generally, "one outside the other," which is the common feature of both. Yet space and time themselves are not an object of sensation, and cannot be passively met in intuition; they are the conditions of possibility of intuition itself, and of our ability to perceive distinct empirical items.

In other words, in the process of intuiting, the human subject receives the material from outside and projects upon it the form that makes it into an intuition. The subject is thus involved in the most basic stage of cognition, the one that supplies the empirical building blocks for its further stages. This means that *there is neither an immediate sense perception, nor a totally chaotic one.* Every perception is mediated *from the outset* by elements of minimal order, an order that derives from the human subject's mode of perception. The subject thus projects its own patterns onto the basic shape of the objective world as an empirical world in time and space. And this entails a first, partial realization of the Copernican thesis already in the act of intuition and prior to the entry of conceptual thinking (the "understanding") into the picture.

So the Copernican reversal starts already on the level of intuition: this point is of great importance to Kant. To support it he has to show that space and time are, on one side, a priori, yet on the other, they are not concepts of the understanding but forms of our intuition (what he calls "pure intuitions"). Kant supports this doctrine in two lines of argument that can be named direct (progressive) and indirect (regressive). (Kant's own titles are "The Metaphysical Explication" and "The Transcendental Explication" of space and time.)

The Direct ("Metaphysical") Explication

(1) The a priori character of space is first of all seen in the fact that it cannot be derived by an inductive generalization from a multitude of spatial locations; for, in order to identify these particular items as spatial, that is, as existing one outside the other and all outside us, we must already use the general concept of space we were supposed to deduce. "Thus the representation of space cannot be obtained from the relations of outer appearance through experience, but their outer experience is itself first possible only through this representation" (A23/B38).

Apparently this is a very broad argument, relevant against empiricism and positivism in general: in order to identify a certain particular as illustrating a general quality, we need to already have a concept of that quality. Yet more specifically, and less overtly, I think Kant is targeting here Leibniz's view of relative space. Leibniz denied the view of space as a kind of container, shaped as a constant grid of coordinates into which events and entities are fitted. This view assigns to each entity a unique constant location, which makes it possible to determine in an absolute way which entity is in motion and which is at rest. Following Descartes, Leibniz argued that movement in space is nothing but a change of one's relative position; hence, strictly speaking we cannot say that the carriage moves and the tree is at rest, nor the opposite, only that their relative position has changed; and space is a derivative of these relations. Kant aims his argument against empiricism and Leibniz alike, and goes back to Newton's view of space as absolute; yet he no longer sees space as a thing in itself, but as a necessary a priori form of human intuition.

(2) Reinforcing this conception is a second argument Kant draws from a mental experiment: "One can never represent that there is no space, although once can very well think that there are no objects to be encountered in it" (A24/B38). In other words, we can mentally abstract from all the objects in our spatial experience, but are incapable to abstract from the representation of space itself. Hence the representation of space is a priori and precedes the object (which also means that space is absolute space). The reliance on a mental experiment emphasizes that we are here concerned with our capability and incapability as humans. This important point underlies the whole theory of intuition. The Transcendental Aesthetics makes claims not about the structure of being in itself, but about the structure and conditions of the limited human subjects that we are. Space (as well as time) is the primary condition for any sensible representation we might have; but space itself is neither a thing within the world nor outside it. Rather, a primordial representation derived from the nature of the subject, space is the necessary framework of all our empirical intuitions from which the objective world of experience is constituted. As such—as a subjective yet universal condition—it endows the outer world with the specific character of spatiality, and subjects it to the laws of geometry.

Since the Kant literature often confuses his attitude to his predecessors on the issue of space, we might summarize it in short. Leibniz stood for relative space and saw spatial relations as *phenomena bene fundata* (well-founded phenomena). Newton stood for absolute space and regarded it as a real being.[7] Kant accepts Newton's image of an absolute space, but argues it is not a real entity but the form of human intuition. Thus Kant opposes Newton on the matter of the reality of space and Leibniz on the matter of its relativity. Space is an ideal, subjective form, but as such it is shaped as a system of absolute coordinates.

(3 – 4) It remains to be shown that the representation of space is not a universal concept (of the understanding) but a mode of intuition, and thus is an a priori *that is specific to intuition*. Kant points out that space is a singular whose parts exist *within* it, whereas a universal concept subsumes its particular items *under* it. A universal concept (like "horse") subsumes under itself a plurality of different items (like Bucephalus and Rocinante), whereas the representation of space does not allow of many different spaces, only of many homogeneous parts (regions) in the same singular space. This is also seen in the different relation that exists in each case between unity and multiplicity. In discursive (conceptual) thinking this is the relation between particulars subsumed under a common quality, and in intuitive representation it is the relation between the whole and part. From the above it follows that perceiving space is a perception of a singular setup and not of a universal concept, and thereby it is an intuition, albeit pure, and not conceptual thinking. (A similar explication is given to the representation of time.)

The Indirect (Regressive or "Transcendental") Explication

The direct explication of space (and time) is supported by a regressive argument that highlights their ideality. The strategy of a regressive argument is to validate a proposition or a theory by

7. To be more precise, as God's *sensorium*, which for created beings is entirely real.

showing that it alone can explain the possibility of some given fact or situation that is admitted as undeniably true.[8] Kant starts with the evident existence of apodictic natural sciences, and asks what makes them possible. If we find a theory that explains this possibility (and if it alone does so) then the theory must be admitted as true, even if, on the surface, it may appear bizarre or absurd. Now, says Kant, the image of space is not only a necessary framework of empirical intuition, it can also be made the object of a special a priori intuition that looks at space itself and studies the pure laws and relations embodied in it: this is the origin of pure geometry. But in order for geometry to be the universal and necessary science it is, it must be pure, not empirical, and relate to space not as a real object but as an a priori structure of the mind, that does not claim to represent things-in-themselves but only to serve as formal framework of whatever the outer senses perceive. In a word, only the features of space as studied in the direct explication are capable to explain the apodictic power of geometry, and this reinforces their validity.

A similar argument concerns time. Time is the form of intuiting our inner states (approximately what the empiricists called "reflexion"). Time's characteristic structure—a sequence of units that follow each other unidirectionally—is the transcendental origin of the theory of numbers (arithmetic). Arithmetic is possible as rigorous science only due to the facts that (1) we have a representation of time that we can intuit a priori and explicate the relations of sequentiality that compose it, and (2) because thereby we study not some real object or thing in itself, but a basic form of the mind.

At the same time there is a notable asymmetry between time and space. Time is more comprehensive, since some phenomena

---

8. In the philosophical jargon this type of argument is called "Transcendental Arguments," a name inspired by Kant. But to avoid confusion between this generalized logical procedure and Kant's substantive (and specific) use of "transcendental" in the Critique, I use the word "regressive."

are given in time and not in space (e.g., mental states and events), whereas no phenomena are given in space and not in time. Actually, the perception of items in space is also subject to the form of inner time in which it takes place. This will have important consequences in many key issues, like causality, empirical psychology, and the question of immortality.

The most outstanding conclusion that derives from these deliberations is the dependence of space and time on the human subject: "if we remove our own subject, or even only the subjective constitution of the senses in general, then all the constitution, all relations of objects in space and time, indeed space and time themselves would disappear" (B59).[9]

The human subject can intuit only through the senses, and sensation is possible only as mediated by the forms of time and space that originate in our mind, and function as primary conditions for the existence of objective phenomena in human experience. The latter notion assumes—the assumption will be grounded later on—that human experience contains sufficient elements that provide it with order, universality, and necessity, in virtue of which it is shaped as an objective experience rather than as a bunch of accidental associations, and the first basis for that are time and space. This allows Kant to say that his doctrine upholds the *empirical reality* of time and space no less than their *transcendental ideality*. In other words, Kant's teaching gives a new philosophical interpretation to the spatiotemporal character of our world, an interpretation that neither abolishes nor in the least diminishes the reality of the empirical world, and certainly does not present it as illusion. The world we know by scientific experience remains unchanged even after it has been metaphysically reinterpreted in terms of Transcendental

9. This striking affirmation sounds bolder than it actually is. It does not say that removing the subject would lead to nothingness, but that it would erase all spatiotemporal relations and law-governed features that make up the objectivity of the empirical world.

Idealism. What changes is the *meaning* of objectivity, or empirical reality, which now stands under a different philosophical light and worldview.[10]

Thus the Copernican reversal is expressed already in the domain of intuition. But this is only a first, ground-laying stage. The main reversal occurs in the work of the understanding.

The Transcendental Logic: The Categories as the Foundations of Objects

In the next stage Kant passes from the theory of intuition to the theory of thinking, that is, logic. Kant emphasizes he means pure logic and not psychological facilitators or auxiliaries; and within pure logic he draws a cutting line, one of the most important in the Critique, between general (formal) logic and what he names transcendental logic.

General (formal) logic is a set of rules for using the understanding in all its tasks. These rules apply to all possible objects of thought without distinction. General logic is interested in the formal relations between the objects of thought, and completely disregards their content and whether they exist or not. Therefore its rules apply equally to real and imaginary objects, as well as to contentless symbols. Because of its maximal level of abstraction, general logic serves as supreme legislation (canon) and necessary condition for all acts of thinking. There can be no valid thinking without observing its rules, yet this is only a necessary but not a sufficient condition of truth. Synthetic, nontautological statements require further truth conditions: not

10. Another explanation of the Kantian thinker's empirical realism can be found in this quote from the A version: "In all the tasks that may come before us in the field of experience, we treat those appearances as objects in themselves" (A393). This does not mean the appearance is indeed a thing in itself, but that it is empirically real, even if the source of its objectivity is ideal. Therefore, it is possible, and required, to make a difference, in the realm of experience, between a real appearance (a lake, for example) and pictures, dreams, or illusions of lakes.

only the agreement of a thought with itself according to the law of noncontradiction, but also the agreement of the thought with the object—and, first of all, its agreement with a set of further logical forms *by virtue of which it is an object.*

In a trivial sense, everything we think of is an object of our thought, since thinking is intentional and always oriented toward something. Yet there is a vital difference between a merely intentional object, which could be anything that crosses our mind, and an object in the sense of a real entity in the world. Hence Kant assumes a special logic he calls transcendental, whose rules apply not indifferently to any object of thought, but specifically to the thinking of real objects. This logic is not meant to replace the formal, analytic logic. Quite the contrary, it is necessarily subject to the latter, but adds to it an additional layer of conditions by which alone one can think real empirical objects. For example, in order to think a real event in nature—as distinct from illusion or imagination—we must think it as a member in a universally determined causal chain in which it is both a consequence and a cause: this is not required in formal logic, which treats its object the same way whether it is real, imaginary, or mythological. Transcendental logic is thus *a logic of objects*, or the logic of *objective being* and the discourse that suits it, and not only the logic of a merely noncontradictory, coherent discourse. Thereby it embodies and realizes the idea of the Copernican revolution in the domain of thought.

Analytic and Dialectic

Because of its object-orientation, transcendental logic must necessarily relate to intuitions given by experience, by which alone we can gain access to reality. (This demand itself is one of the conditions of objectivity that this logic sets forth.) Without being applied to intuitions, transcendental logic would be empty and lacking objective import. At the same time, this logic cannot determine the existence and quality of objects that presumably transcend space and time, and of which, therefore, no intuition is possible. Such application will only engender fallacy and delusions. It follows that transcendental logic does not claim to set the conditions of being in general but only of empirical being—that which concerns real objects in *nature*.

Nevertheless, the temptation is great to attribute to the understanding the capability to determine a priori also the existence and features of supernatural entities and of beings in themselves. This, as we have seen, is the main fallacy of dogmatic metaphysics. Against this background Kant divides transcendental logic into two distinct parts: analytic and dialectic. The analytic (the logic of truth) investigates the conditions of objectivity of empirical entities in time and in space—that is, in nature—and has constitutive jurisdiction over them; dialectic—the logic of illusion—transcends the conditions of time and space and pretends in vain to determine the existence and qualities of things in themselves.

The analytic starts with an investigation of *concepts*—the primary concepts of the understanding that Kant names "categories." Then, given this basis, the analytic proceeds to derive a set of *propositions* (or rather, judgments) that develop the kernel of the categories into principles, the first principles of the understanding and of nature.

The Analytic of Concepts

By the analytic of concepts, Kant says, he does not mean the analysis of complex concepts into simpler ones, but a far more radical move: the disassembly or "analysis of the *faculty of understanding itself* in order to investigate the possibility of a priori concepts by seeking them only in the understanding as their birthplace, and analyzing their pure use." As Kant says:

> We will pursue the pure concepts into their first seeds and predispositions in the human understanding, where they

lie ready, until with the opportunity of experience they are finally developed, and [then], liberated from the empirical conditions attaching to them they are exhibited in their clarity by the very same understanding. (A66/B91; I slightly modified the Guyer/Wood translation)

From here and other texts it is clear that those pure conceptual "seeds," and the syntheses they perform, operate in concealment, or at least in partial consciousness. Therefore they have been unknown to their users and to most previous philosophers. (Similarly, in speaking of what he names "pure imagination," Kant calls it "a hidden art in the depth of the human soul" [A141/B180].) We might say Kant is here anticipating the modern view of the unveiling of unconscious mental formations (except that in Kant they are universal, and are not influenced by the subject's personal history).

In line with the Critique's judicial metaphor, Kant distinguishes between two stages in investigating the categories: "what are the facts" (**quid facti**) and "what's the law" (**quid juris**); in other words, he distinguishes between the stage of discovery and the stage of validation. The first, titled "Metaphysical Deduction," unveils a synthetic-logical system of concepts (categories) that *claim* to determine a priori the empirical objects. The second stage, the "Transcendental Deduction," is meant to justify the claim embodied in the categories and show that, and how, it is valid.

The Metaphysical Deduction and the Discovery of the Categories: What Are the Facts of Reason?

Kant criticizes Aristotle for having picked his categories at random. He demands that the primary concepts of the understanding be deduced and exposed systematically, according to a unifying principle. To guide his search for this principle Kant looks for the fundamental and most deeply rooted activity of the understanding: this is the act of unification, or synthesis. Our understanding being discursive, not intuitive, its fundamental activity consists not in grasping or conceiving anything directly, but in connecting (unifying) the particulars of perception and/ or of thinking, so as to create a certain type of synthetic unity between them. The synthesizing work of the understanding is not one of many mental activities but underlies them all, as their enabling condition. An act of synthesis occurs throughout the whole range of our perception and thinking, not only in conceptual thinking and objective knowledge, but in any perception that combines different data, including associative knowing and acts of imagination (and also, as seen above, in the foundations of mathematics). Synthesis also underlies all acts of disassembly or analysis, since the understanding can take apart only that which it had previously combined. But while the ingredients connected by a synthesis may derive from any source, including sensation, the connection itself cannot be drawn from experience. "Among all representations, combination is the only one that is not given through objects, but can be executed only by the subject itself, since it is an act of its self-activity" (B130).

Here Kant takes a further step, asking how synthesis itself is possible. What function of the subject generates it (and thus stands at the understanding's origin)? His answer: this is the function of self-consciousness. The subject, conscious of itself as an identical "I" to which a manifold of representations is given, ascribes the ingredients of this manifold to itself in the first person singular—that is, as its own representations—thereby connecting them to each other and endowing them with unity of a certain kind. The unity granted the items of the manifold can be of different sorts—logical or intuitive, associative or objective, imaginary or subject to objective laws—but it always, in the last analysis, derives from the unity of the "I think" that is its subject. Thereby the idealist interpretation of synthesis is restated, and, following the Aesthetics, a further major layer is laid expressing the Copernican revolution.

Synthesis as Judgment

Focusing on the narrow meaning of the understanding as thought by concepts, Kant finds that behind every connection of two or more concepts there is an act of judgment. Judgment is the primary form assumed by synthesis in the domain of conceptual thinking and discourse.[11] Hence, says Kant, one can relegate all acts of the understanding to acts of judgment, and even present the understanding in general as the *faculty for judging* (A69/B94). The emphasis here is not on the propositional content of the judgment—not on the substantive claim it makes—but on the act of *making* (performing) the judgment, which takes us back to the role of the subject. To judge that S is P means to connect two or more concepts in one consciousness and to unify them by the unity of that consciousness. This is Kant's idealist theory of judgment, as opposed to the Platonic view of logical relations existing in themselves between propositions and other logical entities. Everyone would allow that the judgment connects the subject-concept S to the predicate-concept P by mediation of the copula (S *is* P). The question is what hides behind the copula and what the nature of the connection is. According to the traditional view, the connection between the grammatical subject and predicate exists in itself as within an independent logical space, while the judgment only copies or represents this connection in thought and language. Kant argues that the judgment creates the very connection, and that at work behind the linguistic sign of the copula is the unifying activity of the subject. In other words, the subject as consciousness does not merely *face* the sentence "S is P" externally, like someone who represents a unit of discourse existing

---

11. Moreover, judgments of the understanding are mediated knowledge, because they apply to the objects of intuition not directly, but only through the mediation of a concept. (This is another expression of the fact that our understanding is discursive and not intuitive.)

in itself; rather, the subject is the one *performing* the judgment, and thus mediating the connection between the elements of the sentence by ascribing them both to its own unity of consciousness. Through that mediation the subject *constitutes* the logical connection in question and the very unit of discourse.

This analysis gives Kant the guiding thread he was looking for. Since,

> the same function that gives unity to the different representations **in a judgment** also gives unity to the mere synthesis of different representation **in an intuition**, which, expressed generally, is called the pure concept of understanding. The same understanding, therefore, and indeed by means of the very same actions through which it brings the logical form of judgment into concepts by means of the analytical unity, also brings a transcendental content into its representations by means of the synthetic unity of the manifold in intuition in general, on account of which they are called pure concepts of the understanding that pertain to objects a priori; this can never be accomplished by universal logic. (A79/B104–5)

Since the understanding exhibits its activity in judgments, we must examine the various forms and uses of judgment, first in general (formal) logic, which is analytic, and, on this background, also in transcendental logic, which is synthetic. Both these systems, each in its own way, embody one and the same set of intellectual root functions from which they branch off, so there is a symmetry and affinity between the two. Consequently, the list of forms of judgments of formal logic, which is already well-known from the history of logic and philosophy, recalls the list of pure categories and serves as a clue for bringing them to light.

I cannot discuss all the details of Table 2, but will add a few remarks:

1. The expression "S is P" may assume several forms, according to the logical quantity, quality, relation, and modality. Thus the judgment "all the French like wine"

Table 2. The Forms of Judgment and the Categories

	Form of Judgment	Example	Category
Quantity	Universal	Every S is P	Unity
	Particular	There is/are S which is/are P	Plurality
	Singular	Napoleon is P	Totality
Quality	Affirmative	S is P	Reality
	Negative	S is not P	Negation
	Infinite	S is "not-P"	Limitation
Relation	Categorical	S is P	Substance and accident
	Hypothetical	If q then r	Cause and effect
	Disjunctive	S is either P1 or P2 or P3	Community (reciprocity)
Modality	Problematic	[it is possible that] S is P	Possibility (and impossibility)
	Assertoric (propositional)	[indeed] S is P	Existence (and nonexistence)
	Apodictic	[necessarily] S is P	Necessity (and contingency)

is universal in quantity, affirmative in quality, categorical in its relation, and assertoric in its modality. The judgment "Jean-Pierre doesn't like wine" is singular in its quantity, negative in quality, categorical and assertoric in its relation and modality, and so on. Thus there can be crosses between several classes, but the basic patterns are constant. These twelve basic patterns of judgment ("the dozen tribes of Israel," mocked the satirists) Kant drew from the traditional books of logic after rearranging them to suit his needs.

2. Although called a "deduction," the passage from the form of judgment to the corresponding category is not really deductive. It rather seems to involve an intuitive leap, based on the affinity between the two contents and

assisted by observing the facts of reason. Some philosophers, starting with Fichte, saw this as a flaw, but to Kant this is a consequence of the finitude of reason. Since we have no self-particularizing intellect, our search for the categories can be only heuristic: the guiding principle tells us where to look, but then there is the actual looking—the act of discovery performed by an intuitive move aimed at the "facts" of reason (i.e., primordial elements inhering in rational activity as such).

3. These facts of reason can have no further explanation. In this respect, the categories' specific contents, as well as their number, are rigid and nontransparent data existing in reason itself (B145–46).

4. The categories do not exhaust all the object-constituting concepts of the understanding, but only their absolutely first layer. Based on these "primary" concepts a whole inventory of "derived" synthetic a priori concepts (power, motion, matter, event, change, etc.) can be worked out. Although they play a vital role in physics and other empirical sciences, and serve equally as a priori conditions of the object and its knowledge, the Critique does not elaborate the derived pure concepts because, says Kant, it deals only with fundamentals.

5. Implied in all categories, especially those relating to reality, existence, possibility, and necessity, is the proviso that they are used in their transcendental or meta-empirical meaning alone, which applies exclusively to empirical beings in space and time and not to things in general. In this sense, the concept of reality (*Realität*) alludes to the rigid, involuntary, and passively received character of sensation; the concept of possibility means there exist valid natural processes that might engender the entity S according to causal laws; and the concept of actuality (*Wirklichkeit*) indicates that S actually exists or has actually occurred. As for the meta-empirical sense of

necessity, it seems to add nothing to actuality; it explicates only one of its conditions, namely, that every actual
existent exists by the necessity of natural laws. (This will
be one of the sources of Kant's natural determinism.)

The Transcendental Deduction: Validating the Categories

The Metaphysical Deduction of the categories presented a
system of synthetic-logical elements (categories) that *claim*
to determine a priori the shape of empirical objects and the
foundations of scientific experience. The Transcendental
Deduction—the heart of Kant's argument in the Analytic—aims
to explain why this claim is justified.

According to the legal metaphor, the former discussion deals
with the question of facts, and the latter with the question of
law. Actually, however, the two discussions are not completely
separate. The Transcendental Deduction uses insights that
have already served the deduction of the categories, and vice
versa. In particular, both share the view that (1) the "I," as self-
consciousness, is what connects the ingredients of synthesis in
all its varieties; (2) that the function of connection is the fundamental act of the understanding; and (3) that this understanding, as the principle of synthesis in general, works (even if unno-
ticeably) wherever a synthesis of *any* kind takes place, including
between the ingredients of intuition, imagination, association,
and so on. As Kant says: "all combination, whether we are conscious of it or not, whether it is a combination of the manifold
of intuition or of several concepts, and in the first case, either
of sensible or non-sensible intuition, is an action of the understanding" (B130). Thereby two principles have been established:
first, that the understanding penetrates all other functions of
knowledge and mind and actually makes them possible, since
all are built on syntheses, and second, that the ultimate source
of the understanding is the unity of the "I think."

From here it can be anticipated that, directly or indirectly, the rules of the "I think"—or the patterns of its activity, the categories—would be expressed in every synthesis the mind performs and would invisibly dominate also nonobjective (and subobjective) combinations of representations.

The Deduction is not built as a single continuous argument, and it assumes different versions in Editions A and B, and in the *Prolegomena*.[12] Nevertheless, it is possible to reconstruct from these texts a set of philosophical analyses, not immediately visible, and to map the outline of their underlying argument(s).

The movement of the Deduction branches off into two procedures, progressive and regressive, that share a similar basic structure. Each starts from an evident datum and inquiries into what makes it possible. One procedure (call it "progressive") starts from the datum of self-consciousness (the "I think"), and the other (call it "regressive") starts from the fact that we have apodictic natural sciences. Although each of these starting points is at first investigated for itself and in its own specific terms, it turns out in the end, not without surprise, that *each makes the other possible*. In this way a positive, or benign circle of reciprocal grounding is founded: the unity of the object is enabled by the identity of the subject, and vice versa.

Paradoxically, both procedures use Hume's skeptical arguments, while denying the assumption at their base. Hume had argued (and according to Kant, demonstrated), that no rule, law, or connection between phenomena can be universal and necessary if derived from experience. At best, experience can give us probabilistic regularity but not rigorous universality, and only associative—that is, contingent—but not necessary connections

---

12. By "deduction" Kant does not refer to deductive logic in its geometrical model. Actually, Kant argues at length (in his Transcendental Doctrine of Method) against this deductive-geometrical model (championed by Descartes, Spinoza, and their followers) and claims that it should be banished from the realm of philosophy altogether. The word "deduction" refers to the Latin idiom *de-ductio* in its literal sense, i.e., guiding (and the guiding of thought) from one thing to another.

between phenomena. And since Hume believed (wrongly, according to Kant), that we have no other cognitive source but experience, he had to replace logical necessity with psychological habituation in explaining the world. From a pragmatic point of view this may be sufficient, but metaphysically it follows that no connection in nature is evident and permanent, neither causality nor substantiality or reciprocity, and therefore, as the young Hume had realized with anxiety and melancholy, although the world appears to us to be ordered and connected, there is nothing to prevent it from being at bottom disintegrated and unstable, a world in which almost everything can link up with everything else or be separated from it, and therefore cannot be expected to possess any objective, rigorously determined state of affairs.

In a parallel way, Hume also attacked the idea of the identity of the "I." Here too, says Hume, we may only rely on experience (in this case, inner experience, or empirical reflection), and this experience exhibits only an ongoing sequence of discrete subjective events, but not a permanent and identical subject of these events. Every act of empirical reflection presents me with some impression—anger, joy, heat, desire, and so on—which at that moment occupies the center of my consciousness, and I can also become aware of my consciousness of it. Yet these are all momentary units without a common substrate or substance—like theater actors who enter and exit a nonexisting stage.[13]

The Transcendental Deduction is meant, as an important byproduct, to meet both of Hume's skeptical arguments. It does so by working in the two directions mentioned above, the regressive and the progressive.

The Regressive Argument

To understand Kant's point of departure in the regressive argument we must remember he was working at the height of the

---

13. Hume, *Treatise of Human Nature*, 1.4.6, "On Personal Identity."

modern scientific revolution, when Galileo's and Newton's physics looked no less evident than pure mathematics, the science
that, from time immemorial, had been seen and accepted as the
ultimate model of scientificity. This allowed Kant to state that
at long last we possess, as a cultural-historical fact, an empirical natural science whose laws and explanations are valid ev-
erywhere and at all times without exception. Kant was unable
to imagine that someone might *seriously* deny this. As we saw
above, he understood Hume as trying to prove the failure and
impossibility not of natural science, but of metaphysics. Moreover, within the new science, from Kepler and Galileo to Newton, there operate first physical principles—sometimes known
as the "postulates of science"—like the principle of inertia, the
equality of action and reaction, the principle of unilateral causality, and the crucial principle that nature lends itself to mathematization. These and their like make up a latent "pure science
of nature" that operates at the bottom of empirical science and
makes it universally valid. So Kant was confident that he could
start from the evident statement that a universal and necessary
science of nature actually exists.

But if so, how are we to explain its possibility? Here Kant
adopts the conclusion of the empiricists, especially Hume, who
showed that once we admit the empiricist doctrine that claims
that all elements of knowledge derive exclusively from experience, we must conclude that no necessary connections are possible between natural objects and events, only contingent and
associative links. Hence, the assumptions of empiricism fails to
account for the possibility of apodictic science—and this, says
Kant, testifies to a major flaw in empiricism and the collapse of
its central doctrine.

The only coherent way to explain the possibility of science is
to recognize that the understanding contains *original* a priori
elements that do not derive from the senses, and that these elements *precondition empirical experience itself.* This implies
that the foundations of objectivity (universality and necessity)

originate in the human understanding, whose own source inheres in self-consciousness—and this is no other than the thesis
of the Copernican revolution.

The old conception of knowledge as a copy of the object is
unable to justify claims about the object, or to make any a priori
knowledge possible, unless we assume a divine mediation between knowledge and the world, as did Descartes and Leibniz.
Yet Kant, who refutes the proofs of God's existence, must reject
such a transcendent solution as an illusion.[14] Hence, the only way
to explain necessary relations in nature and science is to anchor
their source in the human mind rather than in God, and not in
man's sensible apparatus but in metaphysical concepts and principles that depend on his self-consciousness. The Kantian thesis
about the constitution of nature through the process of knowledge allows us to have a priori knowledge of several types of necessary connections working in nature, since the understanding
that sets out to know nature is the same that had constituted
them in the first place. In other words, the understanding thereby
knows not something external but its own basic structure.

The moves of the regressive argument can be schematically
summarized as follows:

1. *We possess a pure science of nature* (this is a primary
   given that is considered irrefutable). From here one concludes by a direct inference from actuality to possibility:

14. In Descartes's philosophy, the images in the mind are representations
of an external reality, while the "natural light" enables us to cognize this reality
and know its rules. The "natural light" was given us by God, whose goodness
ensures that we will not be deceived. Kant could not turn to this transcendent
deus-ex-machina solution, not only because his teaching puts God's existence
in serious doubt, but also, more fundamentally, because the Critique is based
on the autonomy, however limited, of reason, and its main task is to explicate
the immanent world and possibilities of the human being, who replaces God—
the deity that cannot be proved—as the authority and measure of all things, in
knowledge as well as morals.

2. *A pure science of nature is possible.* At this point an extensive epistemological inquiry is conducted, concerning the difference between a priori and empirical knowledge, the meaning of objectivity, and the conditions by which alone necessary connections between representations are possible. This inquiry contains the main philosophical content of the argument, and is summarized by the statement:

3. *A pure science of nature is possible if and only if the understanding legislates to nature.*

From 2 and 3 we get:

4. *The understanding legislates to nature* (the Copernican thesis).

Some have complained that Kant presents a circular argument. Apparently, he proves the universality and necessity of science based upon the Copernican thesis, and proves the validity of the Copernican thesis based upon the universality and necessity of the sciences. The way we analyzed the argument shows this is not the case. The Copernican thesis is justified not by the pure science of nature but by *its success in explaining its possibility*, which is a common and valid way of justifying a theory. The problem with the regressive argument seems to lie elsewhere, not in its formal structure but in its substantive point of departure: Kant failed to take seriously the challenges to the apodicticity of science when he assumed it as an unshakably given "fact." For this reason, in the final analysis, the regressive argument is only secondary in the overall deduction and needs reinforcement from its ultimate agreement with the progressive argument.

Kant sees a further support (though not a sufficient proof) of the Copernican thesis in the Critique's success to spell it out in a detailed and full apparatus of categories and principles of science, which realize the thesis in a complete and coherent system. Without this detailed realization the thesis would remain bizarre (not to say outlandish, especially for the common understanding) and utterly abstract. One might think here of a detective or archaeologist who, based on an independent source, knows with certainty that some action has taken place (the cousin did it!), but cannot explain how and through which intermediary stages it came to be. Finding such explanation reinforces the theory and turns the evidence from abstract to concrete.

The Conditions of Possibility of Nonscientific Experience

On the way to the progressive argument (and again in its end) Kant opens another line of inquiry, asking about the conditions of the possibility of any experiencing in general, and not specifically of the natural sciences. Here the starting point is the obvious but unexplained fact that we have a multitude of sensible experiences of all kinds and shapes, and the question now is what makes *them* possible. The aesthetics has already set up two such kinds of conditions, sensual stimuli and the forms of intuition, space, and time. However, these are necessary but not sufficient conditions. In theory, these conditions would be fulfilled even if our mind would be flooded with a jumble of sensible materials that do not amount to any shaped picture of experience. Yet such a situation is impossible—not because it does not fulfill the conditions of space and time, but because it fails to obey *further* elements of order that anticipate the categorizing work of the understanding. Actually, Kant claims, an amorphous muddle of perceptible materials would only overwhelm the mind without becoming experience even in the everyday, prescientific sense (A111). Yet, as said, such chaos is impossible,[15] and what excludes it is the fact that the empirical elements in our experiencing are anchored in transcendental elements.

---

15. Excepting certain states of delirium and brain damage.

This means, among other things, that on the precategorizing level there are lower forms of syntheses that precede the work of the categories but take their rule from them. This is particularly spelled out in edition A.

The Deduction in Edition A:
The Hierarchy of Syntheses

Kant stresses that there is only one objective world of experience. Insofar as parts of our subjective experiences are objectified with the help of the categories, they join the unity of one and only world of experience (as known by science). But, for the objective synthesis of science to occur, it must be preceded by lower, prescientific syntheses that take place on the level of perception and imagination. These lower, but equally necessary syntheses provide the top synthesis with material and infrastructure in a way that *tacitly anticipates* and meets in advance the conditions and constraints set by the categories, and makes them fit for unification.

This means that even without (or before) being objective, our subcategorical perceptions and imaginations are latently already governed by the conditions of the top cognitive synthesis that builds the unity of the experienced world.

Edition A illustrates this by sketching a hierarchy of three layers of synthesis:[16]

1. *Apprehension*—All the representations of intuition arise within the inner sense, that is, within time; and as such

---

16. A97–110. This discussion is sometimes called "the subjective deduction," a somewhat misleading title. Kant says he is taking these mental processes "not in their psychological but in their transcendental characterization." (As such, the text in A was actually meant to present a hierarchy of *objectifying* syntheses "which make possible . . . all experience as an empirical product of understanding" [A98].) Still, since early readers tended to understand this text as promoting a subjective idealism or psychologism, which Kant strongly disowned, he dropped the A Deduction from the revised edition of the book.

they are discrete items. But a manifold of discrete representations will never give us knowledge unless they are
brought into unification. "In order for **unity** of intuition
to come from this manifold . . . , it is necessary first to
run through and then to take together this manifold-
ness, which action I call the **synthesis of apprehension**"
(A99). A synthesis of apprehension exists in every daily
experience that perceives shaped forms and patterns—a
cottage, an apple, a stream of water, or a musical theme.
Equally, a synthesis of apprehension exists in the pure
construction of mathematical entities (a line, a number).

2. *Reproduction and association*—Apprehension depends
on a synthesis of reproduction, in which the imagination
brings back to consciousness a previous experience or
datum that is no longer present to it. Since the representations arise in the mind in a consecutive order, one after
the other, only one of them can occupy the center of consciousness at any given time. Hence, "if I were always to
lose the preceding representation . . . from my thoughts
and not reproduce them when I proceed to the following
ones, then no whole representation, and none of the previously mentioned thoughts, . . . could ever arise" (A102).
In order to unify the manifold into a definite form,
we need, time and again, to make present the former
thoughts that have been thrust into the past. This action
is performed by the imagination, which is the power of
making the absent present.

Kant sees the laws of association as a privileged example of the synthesis of reproduction. According to these
laws, if one or more representations habitually appear
to me together, then later, when I perceive one of them,
my mind will recall the others too. Kant argues that the
law of association (which he calls the law of reproduction) is not primary but depends on prior conditions.
Above all, there must already exist a certain tacit affinity
between the components of an association in order to

make it occur. In other words, although an association is a subjective and accidental perception, it cannot take place in *any* manner, nor between any two perceptions, but only between perceptions that lend themselves to being associated. If so, then underlying the synthesis of the imagination there must be a transcendental synthesis already at work, which tacitly shapes the representations and their possible combinations in line with the demands of the categories. This synthesis is the work of the "pure imagination," a mental faculty that the philosophical tradition had not been aware of, but Kant affirms its existence and assigns it a key role in his doctrine (as he already did in the matter of "schematism").

3. *Recognition*—Recognition is another necessary condition though not a sufficient one. "Without recognition that that which we think is the very same as what we thought a moment before, all reproduction in the series of representation would be in vain. For it would be a new representation in our current state, which would not belong at all to the act through which it had been gradually generated, and its manifold would never constitute a whole, since it would lack the unity that only consciousness can obtain for it" (A103).

Hence, as an anchor for all the previous syntheses we need a synthesis of re-cognition, which allows us to identify the series of alternating representations as belonging to the same matter and as being thought by the same mind (subject); and this self-consciousness, even when it is not clear and explicit, is the highest condition for the many representations to be unified into a common representation (as in apprehension, etc.); thereby it conditions all the other syntheses. The top synthesis is no longer the work of the imagination, although it needs its indispensable assistance, but the work of the pure "I think" that works through concepts in agreement with patterns of the categories.

The above discussion illustrates how the unification of empirical objects in ordinary apprehension and association is neither primary, nor open to any arbitrary combination (as in Hume), but is itself made possible (hence, also constrained) by a transcendental synthesis, which the pure imagination performs in submission to the guidelines of the categories. Thus *the categories are indirectly responsible also for the possibility of association* and the other lower levels of perception.

The Progressive Argument

The main pillar of the Deduction, the anchor that holds everything together, is the concept of the pure subject—the "I think" from which Descartes had already started, but, according to Kant, misunderstood his own discovery. Kant also refers to it as "the transcendental ego" as well as "pure apperception."[17] We have seen above the role of the Kantian "I think" in generating all syntheses and judgments, and as the highest condition not only of objective cognitions but of all perceptions generally. But we have not yet asked, *what are the conditions of the possibility of the "I think" itself?*

This question must be considered a paradox, even an outright scandal, by post-Cartesian philosophy, which takes the "I think" to be absolutely primary and simple (unmediated). Yet Kant, who shuns simples, places this question at the heart of the Deduction. Descartes was right to start from the *cogito* but misinterpreted his point of departure. When Descartes thinks (or writes) the apparently innocuous expression "I think," he is unaware that he already stands at the height of a complex logical-mental process that preceded that statement and makes it possible. The Deduction in its progressive move exposes and explicates this process as a series of conditions.

---

17. In the Leibnizian vocabulary, "apperception" means self-consciousness.

The foundation of the progressive argument is laid down in paragraphs 15 and 16 of the B edition. The famous sentence "The **I think** must be **able** to accompany all my representations" (B132) presents the supreme condition of our thinking and experiencing, that is, of having any representations at all. There can be no experiencing unless it is the experience of some identical subject "which in all consciousness is one and the same" (B132). Kant emphasizes that this reflexive act (or *self*-consciousness) need not always actually occur, but must be always available as a possibility. The condition of my thinking and perceiving is not that I be aware of them at every moment, but that at every moment I could *become* aware of them.

However, the basic datum from which Kant starts is the realization of the "I think," not just its abstract possibility. Such realization recurs in our conscious life whenever someone says (or thinks) "I think." Since no one contests this datum, one may start from it as an evident given, and inquire into what makes it possible. This inquiry combines systematic analysis with phenomenological insights—that is, descriptive statements about the nature of our mental functions—and is summed up in two sets of conditions.

In the first stage it turns out that the realization of the "I think" would not have been possible on the basis of a single thematic representation, but requires that consciousness accompany a manifold of representations and unifies them while asserting its self-identity through them. It is true that a single representation also requires, in principle, the possibility of the consciousness, "I think," but the *realization* of this consciousness is impossible on the basis of a single representation, because the I knows itself only through its connecting acts, and here there is nothing for it to connect. Actually, talk about a single representation is mistaken, and even vacuous, because it relies, as Berkeley argued, on a *post factum* abstraction that severs a particular item from the cluster in which it has originally appeared. A consciousness of a single representation is for us void, since for

representations to exist at all they must be accompanied by the
subject's self-consciousness, which is always the consciousness
of a *connection* between several representations; hence it cannot be realized on the basis of one single representation. Such a
"relation [of a representation to the subject's identity] therefore
does not yet come about by my accompanying each representation with consciousness [of its own], but rather by my *adding*
one representation to the other and being conscious of their synthesis" (B133).

In other words, the ascription by the subject of a representation to itself as its own is never immediate, but is always mediated by a nexus of interconnections, where the nexus itself is
not given beforehand but is *connected* by the subject. Similarly,
the I too is not known to itself immediately, but only through
the identification of itself as the agent that unifies that nexus.
"This thoroughgoing identity of the apperception of a manifold
given in intuition contains a synthesis of the representations,
and is possible only through the consciousness of this synthesis"
(B133). Also: "It is only because I can combine a manifold of
given representations **in one consciousness** that it is possible
for me to represent [i.e., to know, to realize] the **identity of
the consciousness in these representations**" (B133). In other
words, "the **analytical** unity of apperception is only possible
under the presupposition of some **synthetic** one" (B133). "The
thought that these representations . . . **belong to me** means, accordingly, . . . that I unite them in a self-consciousness, or at
least can unite them therein. . . . For otherwise, I would have
as multicolored, diverse a self as I have representations" (B134).

An analytic identity is the direct identity of a thing with itself
(Y = Y). Yet the subject does not have a simple, pregiven identity, with which it sets out to perform various synthetic functions; rather, its self-identity is realized only through its typical
activity, which is the synthesis of the manifold—that is, the unification of what is other than itself—and through the recognition of itself as the unifying agent. In this respect, the subject's

identity is not simple but the result of a process; it is an act of self-identification, one that constitutes identity, and not a primary datum.

These are the first phenomenological assumptions of the progressive argument (indeed of the whole Deduction). On one side they use an element of descriptive insight. Kant observes the act of perception, which leads him to partly accept Berkeley's critique of Locke's account of experience.[18] At the same time he also draws systematic conclusions from two assumptions already made in the Metaphysical Deduction of the categories, namely, that (a) the understanding, being discursive, does not directly perceive any contents but only connects them; (b) that the deep root of the understanding lies in the subject's consciousness. From here he infers that if self-consciousness is a connection of particular items, then it knows itself only as and through that connection; from which it follows that an immediate self-consciousness as in Descartes, or Hume's discrete acts of reflection (the actors in a theater) are absolutely impossible.

But this is only the first part of the story. In the following stage it turns out that the conditions we cited above for the possibility of the I think are not sufficient. Not every combination of mental contents allows the subject to recognize itself as identical in the diversity of its representations, but only an *objective* connection, one that constitutes an *object*, or at least, one that lends itself to being transformed, according to fixed rules, into an objective connection. In other words, the subject does not identify itself as merely connecting the manifold; the connection must be such that enables the subject to sharply distinguish

18. Berkeley criticized Locke's theory that knowledge is founded on singular atoms of experience—a red stain, a creaking noise, a rounded shape, etc.—from which we compose ideas of complex entities. Berkeley claimed that even our initial experience comes in bundles of impressions, and the singular impression is a retrospective abstraction. Kant accepts—regarding this specific issue—Berkeley's argument, while denying his assumption that the composition itself is based on experience.

between itself and the world—between subject and object; and that is achieved by applying the categories of real existence to some representations, whereby an ontological opposition is set between merely subjective representations, which belong only to my particular inner movie (my empirical consciousness), and objective combinations that can be ascribed to the unity of a permanent, law-governed world, which faces me as distinct from myself. At the conclusion of the Deduction it thus turns out that the subject cannot reach a consciousness of its identity except through the mediation of a permanent object that is not itself, and through its own role as the agent who unifies that object. But at the start of the Deduction, as the first stage in explicating the structure of consciousness, we only reach the statement that the I can know itself only through unifying a manifold of representations.

The link between the two stages is maintained by the principle that mere unification is not enough. Not *any* unification can mediate the self's identity, only objective unifications can. For a unification of any kind to take place, even at the lower empirical level of perception and association, it is necessary that its ingredients be capable of being unified *also* on the object-building level of the categories. This idea, which was spelled out more broadly in the A Deduction and the pages above, is also contained in the dense text of paragraph 16: "[these] representations (even if I am not conscious of them as such) . . . must yet necessarily be in accord with the condition under which alone they **can** stand together in a universal self-consciousness, because otherwise they would not throughout belong to me" (they would not be coherent with our objective knowledge of the world and with the I's permanent identity [B132–33]). In other words, ascribing the representations to an individual subject presupposes that they can also be ascribed to a universal consciousness, that is, be capable of cohering with each other according to the rules of the categories and constitute a unified objective world. To be sure, there is no need that all of them do so; some representations may well appear in subjective, accidental inter-connections. But if we are to say that one consciousness unites them too, it is imperative that this consciousness be able to unite them *also* in modes that are not specific to its accidental stand-point but express universal and necessary connecting rules.

This demand presupposes that the empirical representations alternating in our mind *lend* themselves to objective connections, and in this way, pure self-consciousness determines the shape of *the basic givenness itself.* Not all modes of being-given, and not all forms of experiencing, are possible if there is to be self-consciousness. Only that mode of givenness is possible, which holds the capacity of meeting the demands of the categories and the a priori principles of the understanding. Moreover, since Kant's concept of objectivity implies a universal and necessary synthesis of perceptions (or the judgments thereof), every uni-fication in one consciousness tacitly contains the distinction be-tween objective states of affairs and merely subjective orders of time and representation. Hence it is necessary that all the repre-sentations that arise in our mind be *transformable* from the sub-jective to the objective level, that is, severed from the accidental stream of our particular inner experience and reintegrated in a new synthesis that constitutes a unified real world that confronts us. This transformation follows fixed forms that the Metaphysical Deduction has already discovered and exhibited (and which will be later developed in the "Transcendental Principles"); therefore, in order for self-conscience to occur, it is necessary that all repre-sentations, *in their very givenness*, possess certain affinities that match the latent, precategorical imprint of the categories. To say this is no less than stating that the world as known in experi-ence is subject to the a priori demands of the understanding; or, in Kant's suggestive phrase, this explains "the possibility of as it were prescribing the law to nature and even making the latter possible" (B159; *Prolegomena*, para. 36).

Due to the importance of this matter we shall stay with it for a while.

An objectivization of the orders of time and representation occurs fully in science, and, to a certain degree, also in everyday life. When apprehending a waterfall from where I stand I may perceive its parts, changing colors, rapidity, and so on. Yet the categories of substance, causality, and others, allow me to extract the representations from my subjective perspective and reintegrate their relevant input within different orders of time, space, and causality that determine the waterfall's objective relations to the rest of the world and are valid for all observers. Similarly, we perceive the lightning before the thunder, see the top of the tree brushing the sun, and are habituated by other associative combinations that have nothing in common except being contiguous in our subjective experience. The categories of substance, quantity, and especially causality, with the universal laws of nature they support, make it possible to undo the accidental links of representations as they arose in raw perception and rearrange them in objective orders that fit the one world of experience called Nature.

Kant stresses the need for *existence* connectives as a condition for the possibility of self-consciousness. (This is also his argument against solipsism.) Every experiencing must be, at least partially, an experience of the united and coherent world that has already been constituted, otherwise it would split into a plurality of consciousnesses and there will be no experience at all. Free association has no bounds, and were it the only kind of combining representations in one consciousness, there would be no permanence and no necessity in these combinations, not even potentially, and Hume would be right that the word "I" refers to a plurality of discrete reflective acts that have no common identitarian ground. The identity of the I can be realized only because the multiple representations are—or at least *can be*—integrated in the single objective world order that is determined by the subject while separating itself from it. And this requires that the representations themselves contain a precategorical element of permanence that allows to reidentify them and to ascribe to them stable distinctions, just as it requires that the sensible representations contain the potentiality of an objective order that permits us to determine them as belonging to the single unified world. It is only because consciousness, through categories like substance, accident, cause and effect, interaction, and so on, performs such objective connections while ascribing existence to them—and only because the sensible representations lend themselves to such objectifying connections—that the subject is able to know itself and to reassert its identity within the stream of its representations, and say, "I think."

At the conclusion of the Deduction it turns out, for Descartes to be able to say (or write) *cogito*, he must already have had the experience not only of himself, but of some plurality—not a subjective plurality but one that relates to an objective world that is separate from his private mind, and obeys universal and necessary laws prescribed by the pure I through the categories. Thus, not only is the understanding, in working through the categories, capable of "prescribing the law to nature" and making nature itself possible (B159; *Prolegomena*, para. 36), but, mediated by the objective world it has constituted, and facing it as an opposite pole, *consciousness even realizes its own identity as subject.* This is a benign circularity between two poles that make each other possible. The identity of the subject makes possible the unity of the object, *and vice versa*, the unity of the object (the objective world) enables the subject to constitute and realize its identity. The regressive and the progressive arguments thus support each other in a constructive circle, and the Deduction responds in a single (if complex) stroke to Hume's two challenges, concerning objective knowledge and concerning the identity of the subject.

Schematic Presentation

Given the complexity of the progressive argument and its satellite arguments, it is difficult to present its course in a single final scheme. But one can sketch its territory with the following set of propositions (which can also be arranged differently).

PART 1

- *Point of departure: we have a self-consciousness expressed as an identical "I think."*
- All our representations are possible only in relation to this "I think."
- Human understanding, being discursive, does not grasp contents directly but only connects what is given to it.
- The act of connection derives not from experience but from the understanding itself.
- At the root of every connection there stands the unity of self-consciousness (the pure "transcendental subject").
- An identical self-consciousness is impossible on the basis of a single representation.
- [Self-]consciousness can know itself only as the act of connection it is, and only by the mediation of actual connections it performs.
- The "I think" is possible only through connecting the manifold of representations as its own representations.

Interim conclusion: The identity of the "I think" is not given beforehand, but is realized by its action in uniting the manifold.

PART 2

- If all our representations were subjective and accidental, we would have as many units of "I" as we have representations.
- The connections through which the "I" realizes its identity cannot be merely subjective and accidental.
- In order for me to have a stable "I" within the stream of representations, it is necessary that at least *part* of these representations be united through existence connections that are not subject to my subjective time order, but establish the orders of an objective world that is distinct from me.
- Without the opposing pole of an objective world and the existence connections that constitute it (the categories),

I would not even have private, associative connections of representations.

- All modes of perception, even the lowest, are possible only if they are capable of being transformed into categorical connections. Thus, they (and their ingredients) maintain a basic affinity that receives its rule from the categories.
- Thereby, the categories present a further, indirect set of conditions for the possibility of sense perception, in addition to the direct conditions set by space and time.

Final conclusion: Through the categories the a priori understanding dictates its laws to nature and even makes nature itself possible (i.e., the Copernican thesis).

To conclude the analysis of the Deduction, several remarks are in place.

1. In both editions, the Deduction is said to prove that all phenomena in experience "must stand under conditions of the necessary unity of apperception just as in mere intuition they must stand under the formal conditions of space and time" (A110).[19] The forms of time and space are conditions of the possibility of the *particulars* of intuition; and every *combination* of such particulars, whether objective or not, is, in addition, also subject to the a priori conditions of the understanding expressed in the categories. But the parallel is not complete; there is an important difference between the two sets of conditions. Time and space shape the sense perceptions directly and automatically, while the category does so

---

19. In the B version this conclusion is stated otherwise: "Now since all possible perception depends on the synthesis of apprehension, but the latter itself, this empirical synthesis, depends on the transcendental one, thus on the categories, all possible perceptions, hence everything that can ever reach empirical consciousness, i.e., all appearances of nature, as far as their combination is concerned, stand under the categories" (B164–65).

indirectly or tacitly. Every perception must be actually spatialized and temporalized, but does not have to be actually categorized, only to be *capable* of undergoing categorization; which means that every perception is subject to the categories at least *latently* (*in potentia*).

2. Hence, the possibility of the I think does not require complete objectivation. Suffice that *part* of the perceptions have undergone categorization—which gives them necessity and enables them to constitute an independent unified world of objects that faces the I—and that all other perceptions be *convertible* to the same objective world, while still remaining on the level of contingent, associative, or imaginary cognitions. In this way, the Deduction leaves room for combinations of the imagination, dreams, fiction, personal wandering of the mind, as well as aesthetic experiences.

3. It follows from the Deduction that I and the world mutually constitute one another: the unity of the object is the anchor for the identity of the subject, and vice versa. But Kant did not take the all-important further step (which Hegel took) of arguing that the subject's relation to *other* subjects is also an essential condition of self-consciousness (nor did he work out the moral and political implications of such a broader position).

4. Kant describes the pure "I" as transcendental, by which he means that (a) it is not a substance; (b) it is not a process in time; (c) it cannot have predicates; (d) there are no intuitions specifically relevant to it; (e) it is a pure dynamic-logical form; (f) it is not a thing in itself, but the highest condition for all empirical phenomena. Already in its famous appearance in B (para. 16), the "I think" was presented as a kind of "unaccompanied accompaniment" of the representations that cannot itself be accompanied by any further representation—which implies that it evades all thematization and all objectivation, and is

always a subject and never an object. Thereby Kant
seeks to avoid the interpretation of the I think as substance, even as an eternal soul (see later the section on
the "Paralogisms"). On the other hand, every person
has an empirical personality or soul, which is one of the
world's particular phenomena, one that exists in time
(though not in space) and is subject to the categories
and the laws of empirical psychology. This psychological
soul *is* a substance (in the empirical sense: substance as
phenomenon), and as such, like any other phenomenon,
the empirical self is connected and constituted by the
transcendental I. Yet the transcendental I can never be
made a substance, neither empirical nor transcendental,
but evades all objectivation while being the highest condition for them all.

5. In the B edition Kant inserted a section on "The Refutation of Idealism," in order to prove (against Berkeley)
the reality of the outer world in space and to refute Descartes's (and the solipsists') claim that a worldless ego is
possible. The refutation of Idealism is based on the same
logic as the progressive argument (in its second stage),
and by joining the two texts we get approximately the
following: if there is to be an identical self-consciousness
(like the one we actually have), then our mind cannot
contain a merely floating and unstable stream of consciousness. Facing it there must be also a stable and permanent opposite pole in which the subject can find an
anchor for its self-identity. This anchor is provided by the
objective world of experience in space and time, which
distinguishes itself from the accidental junctions of the
subjective stream of consciousness, doing so through the
categories and the necessary existence connections they
establish between phenomena. Thereby the categories
are the necessary conditions not only for the possibility
of objective knowledge and its objects, but also for the

possibility of the identical self-consciousness from which we started.

6. Finally, we are in a position to summarize in three points the profound difference between Kant and Descartes, despite their apparent common starting point: (a) Descartes saw the cogito as a simple, unmediated given that has no previous conditions for its possibility; (b) Descartes presupposed the possibility of a worldless subject; (c) Descartes understood the ego as a substance, even as an eternal soul. Kant in the Deduction refutes the first two claims and sets the ground for refuting the third later in the Dialectic.

Schematism

Under this title Kant raises a wider problem that penetrates all parts of his system. The problem arises from the rigorous duality and hiatus between the senses and the understanding, or more precisely, between receptivity and spontaneity, which are the components of the Kantian synthesis not only in knowledge but also in applying morality to the world of the senses. Without combining these two elements there *is* nothing; but what will account for the success of their unification?

In the final analysis, Kant has no satisfactory answer and must view the fact of the synthesis as contingent, a happy occurrence that reason cannot account for. All we can do is explore the *how* and not the why, that is, discover the intermediary apparatus through which that happy chance, which the Deduction affirms, occurs.[20] From this viewpoint the section on schematism adds nothing *in principle* to the Deduction; but it greatly enriches the picture of the mind's capacities, including the

20. After all, the Deduction had proved that without the possibility of the objective synthesis, even the associative and random experience of the senses would not be possible.

mediating apparatus between the senses and the understanding. In so doing it sheds light on the *pure imagination*, a special faculty that tradition did not recognize, but to which Kant, who believes he has discovered it, assigns a crucial role as the bolt that unites all the elements of perception, the sensible as well as the intellectual.

Pure imagination uses time, the form of intuition, as material for building schemes for the categories. By "scheme" Kant means *the exhibition of a conceptual content within the medium of pure intuition*. In a less rigorous idiom we might say that this is a kind of translation of the category's content into temporal terms. Pure imagination looks at the form of time and shapes it in time patterns that are supposed to exhibit (or embody) the categories. The background assumption here is that the embodiment involves not the loss of any of the category's content, but only changes of the medium in which it is exhibited. As such, the scheme is said to serve as a mediating factor between the matter of sense perception and the categories. Furthermore, the scheme is a condition for the very use of the categories. The category cannot apply directly to empirical intuition, but must undergo schematization, that is, embodiment in a scheme, in order to be meaningful and apt for use. And from the opposite side, the matter of the senses must be ordered and connected in agreement with some temporal scheme (one or more), in order to be able to undergo categorization.

The table of schemes Kant offers is quite intuitive and, as is his custom, divided according to the four groups of categories. In the group of quantity, the scheme of the concept of empirical quantity is *number* (built upon the form of time); that is, the numerical value of the magnitudes intuited in experience links them to the category of pure quantity. In the group of quality, the scheme of the concept of reality is *filled time* (in sensation), while the scheme of the category of negation is *empty time* (empty of all sensation and thought). In the group of relation, the scheme of the concept of substance is the *permanence* of the real in time, that is, its representation as a constant substrate of alterations. The scheme of the category of causality is the *succession* of the real in time according to a law; and the scheme of community (interaction, reciprocity) is the *simultaneity of existence* of the real. In the group of modality, the schemes of possibility, actuality, and necessity are, in that order, the agreement of an object with the *conditions* of time, the existence of an object at a *certain* time, and the existence of an object in *all time.*

From the above it follows that in order to apply the category of quantity, the matter of intuition must possess a numerical magnitude; in order to apply the category of substance, a permanence in time must be represented; to apply the category of causality there must be a law-governed succession in time; and to apply interaction, the scheme of simultaneity must be at work. *The category has nothing to hold on to unless the matter of intuition is first organized by a scheme, and vice versa: without exhibiting the content of the category in the medium of time, we have no way of applying the category to the matter of intuition.* (Of course, all these conditions, set by the schematism, while expressing the Copernican thesis in more detail, also restrict its effective range to the bounds of time, that is, to the immanent empirical world.)

Seen from this angle of schematism, the imagination and the schemes it builds are supposed to mediate the constitution of empirical objects and laws. However, they do not (and are not supposed to) explain the coming together in the final synthesis of the two radically heterogeneous sources, the spontaneous and the receptive.[21] This puzzle has no solution in Kant, who rejects the temptation to place some unknown "common origin" at their root. The schematism only spells out in more detail the cognitive

---

21. Actually, as the schemes are entirely pure elements, they cannot participate in both poles, the receptive and the spontaneous, but should count as belonging entirely to spontaneity.

apparatus of their union, whose *factual* occurrence, as proved by the Deduction, remains a "happy chance."

The Analytic of Transcendental Principles: The "Pure Science of Nature"

The transcendental analytic is divided into two: the analytic of concepts and the analytic of principles. The former deals with categories, which are the ground *concepts* of the synthetic logic, and the latter develops these concepts into *propositions*. These are the synthetic a priori propositions (judgments) whose possibility was linked to the question of metaphysics as science. No wonder, therefore, that here we find most of the basic postulates of modern science as it has taken shape since the scientific revolutions of the seventeenth century, including the principles of the mathematical quantifiability of nature, the dependence on observation, the law of mechanical causality, the law of interaction, and the conservation of a basic physical quantity in nature. For this reason, Kant names his doctrine of principles, with the categories at their base, "a pure science of nature," that is, the a priori foundations of the empirical natural sciences.

Kant defines his set of principles as "rules for the objective use of the categories." The term "objective use" is meant here in the sense of *objectifying* use, the one that constitutes an object. This use is built on the supreme principle that "every object stands under the necessary conditions of the synthetic unity of the manifold of intuition in a possible experience" (A158/B197). In other words, the possibility of an objective entity—the possibility that such an entity would exist in nature and be what it is—depends on complying with a set of prior conditions that must be fulfilled if a synthetic unification of many representations in one consciousness is to take place. And this is none other than asserting the Copernican thesis, which Kant rephrases here in a dry, but precise language packed with implications: "*The conditions of the possibility of experience in general are at the same time conditions of the possibility of the objects of experience*" (A154/B197). Put differently, the a priori *knowledge* conditions under which alone we are able to unite representations in one consciousness and create a scientific, objective world picture are the same as the ontological *existence* conditions under which the objects in that world can *be* what they are, and what our knowledge says they are. From here one can understand the ontological import of the Copernican shift, which determines not only the structure of knowledge but equally the structure of (empirical) being.

Following the categories, the system of Transcendental Principles is divided in four groups. Their titles are quite elaborate, but whether they are called "axioms" or "anticipations" or "analogies" or "postulates," they all do the same work: spelling out the primary apparatus of synthetic a priori judgments.

(A) **The Axioms of Intuition** state that all intuitions are extensive magnitudes. Every intuition is given in time and often in space too, and since space and time are extending systems built as a synthesis of homogeneous components located outside one another, every particular intuition also possesses a certain extensive magnitude. Furthermore, this magnitude can be mathematically determined, since space and time by which they are constructed are equally the origins of mathematics. In this way the Axioms of Intuition make possible the *mathematization of nature*, which is one of the pillars of modern science since Kepler, Galileo, and Descartes. In Kant's words, it is the transcendental principle that ensures the passage from pure mathematics to an applied "mathematics of nature" to which all natural phenomena must submit. What the understanding is here dictating is that all natural phenomena must follow the laws, measurements, and quantitative relations of mathematics (not a self-evident matter). In other words, *the ability of the matter of intuition (sensation, etc.) to be mathematically determined and quantified is an a priori condition of the very possibility of nature and the objects within it.*

(B) This idea finds its complement in the **Anticipations of Perception**. Their principle states that every sensation (without which there can be no objectification) is subject to quantifiable degrees of *intensity*. Here we are dealing with intensive, not extensive magnitudes. For example, in feeling pain or watching a candle burning, our sensation lasts a certain time; but we can also focus on the sensation itself, as if in a timeless instant, and ask what was the *power* or intensity of the pain or the flashing light. Kant's principle states that the degree of intensity must also lend itself to mathematical expression. This widens the principle of nature's mathematical quantifiability to the domain of inner sensation, including empirical psychology and its derivatives.

Notes to the **Mathematical Principles**:

Kant stresses that the content of the mathematical axioms (such as Euclid's) and the primary modes of demonstration cannot be known by the understanding but only by pure intuition. The a priori understanding states only that there can be no object in nature that is not subject to the possibility of mathematization (or, for space, geometrization). But what are the axioms of the geometrical system to which the object is subject—this cannot be discovered by the understanding, but must be derived from pure intuition. (Thereby, perhaps, Kant's theory leaves an opening for using non-Euclidean geometry in physics, even though Kant himself did not come up with such an idea, which to him would have looked outlandish.)

The subjection of nature to the rules and parameters of mathematics is far from being self-evident. Why should the calculations we perform in a purely formal science like mathematics be binding on nature—that is, verified by experience? No formal-logical necessity obtains here, since assuming the opposite involves no logical contradiction. The philosopher must therefore explain why, despite the lack of formal-logical necessity, there is nevertheless a transcendental-logical necessity at work here. This necessity does not flow analytically from the very use of concepts, but derives synthetically from the conditions of uniting representations in one consciousness, and therefore is an a priori condition of our very possibility to think real objects in nature.

This, then, summarizes Kant's message in the Axioms of Intuition. Empirical nature is utterly impossible unless it is mathematically quantifiable, and this is a law not of formal logic, but of the transcendental logic discussed here (which may, at will, be also named synthetic, meta-empirical, or metaphysical).

(C) **The Analogies of Experience** practically occupy the center of the Transcendental Principles. The need for necessary relations between the natural phenomena is determined here as an a priori condition of their possibility. These are the relation of substance, causality, and reciprocal action, all of which are *existence* connections. In other words, in the analogies we no longer consider the conditions of intuition or perception merely, but the conditions of existence of natural phenomena as *actual entities*. And here, too, Kant's answer to Hume is sketched out. Hume's question can be reformulated thus: are the relations between the things we perceive in nature necessary or contingent? To which Kant responds: there is no difference between the existence of these things and the existence of necessary connections between them. The existence of necessary connections is an a priori condition for the existence of a natural world and of actual objects in it.

This is a clear variety of the Copernican thesis. Moreover, the proofs Kant presents of the validity of the principles of substance, causality, and reciprocal action work as a variant of the progressive argument of the Deduction. All three are presented in terms of the relation between subjective and objective orders of time and representation. We experience a certain bundle of perceptions that appear in a certain subjective order of time and of association. The role of objective knowledge is to replace these orders by objective ones that determine the object through universal and necessary laws of a world that is separate from myself, and does not depend on the accidental changes of my perspectives. Kant tries to show that this replacement requires the use of certain types of necessary connection that are determined in accordance with the categories and rephrased in the Analogies.

There are three Analogies of Experience.

First Analogy—the principle of the permanence of substance—"In all change of appearances substance persists, and its quantum is neither increased nor diminished in nature" (B224).

In order to pass from subjective to objective time, one needs to break away from the realm of the transient in general and assume a permanent substrate in relation to which the changes take place and can be measured. This basic principle leads Kant to two conclusions. First is that the background against which one can estimate change is time itself. Time, says Kant, does not pass away, only the appearances in it do. Time is the persisting framework of alteration. Then Kant takes a further step. He develops the concept of time into the notion of duration, which means that some *entity* persists in time and becomes the permanent element and substrate of changes we are seeking. In consequence Kant affirms (like the pre-Socratics, or Descartes) that there is in nature an elementary physical quantity which remains the same in all the physical changes. Kant calls this element "substance" (*Substanz*), which carries also the connotation of matter.

Thereby Kant lays down the a priori basis for the venerated Law of Conservation, which had accompanied modern science since the seventeenth century. Descartes spoke of the conservation of motion, others maintained the conservation of matter, then of energy. Kant does not commit himself to the specific nature of the conserved physical quantity: is it matter? motion? energy? This is an empirical question that philosophy cannot answer a priori. However, the philosopher can determine a priori that, if there is a unified nature, then necessarily its basic physical quantity remains the same in all alterations.

A certain equivocation arises occasionally when Kant speaks of substances in the plural. The empirical changes occurring in a single substance—a tree, a person, a mountain—are subject to a similar rule. It is impossible to perceive changes, certainly not generation and extinction or passing away, unless they are perceived as altering states of something that persists; and this is the substance. Kant says, "everything that is altered is *lasting*, and only its **state changes**" (A187/B230). And, in a somewhat paradoxical phrasing, only the permanent (substance) changes. A person whose skin got tanned has changed, but the white skin did not change, it passed away. (The issue of particular substances leaves open the question of how their concept relates to that of substance in general.)

Second Analogy—the principle of causality (more precisely—of succession in time according to the law of causality)—"all alterations occur in accordance with the law of the connection of cause and effect" (B232).

This is, so to speak, the senior principle, at least historically; and its proof is based on a variant of the progressive argument. Sense perception yields subjective orders of time and representation, and in order to pass on to objective orders, one would usually have to change or reverse the order of time. (The lightning is simultaneous with the thunder and does not precede it, the smoking gun comes before the victim's body, although it was discovered afterward.) For that we need a rule that enables us to determine in each case what is the right temporal order—the one belonging to the objective state of affairs; and this rule derives from the object's causal relations. The principle of causality in its primary role has to determine the correct temporal orders in the unified world; it is a principle for setting the sequence of time in a new order.

More specifically, Kant argues that in order for us to have an objective world—and for nature to be able to exist at all—there must be a conceptual ground on which one can organize the orders of time coherently and consequentially. This ground is called cause, and it determines that of two events represented in perception, one must come before the other in a necessary and irreversible sequence. Kant's principle does not claim to know the *material* features of the cause. Is it a push, a thrust, an attraction, a repulsion, a temptation, or perhaps love or hatred? The a priori principle cannot determine anything material, nor does it need to do so. All it conveys is that there is a necessary and irreversible connection between phenomena that can be known and formulated by a constant rule. This is the conceptual core of causality, of which the material characteristics are learned from experience. On this basis one can reconstruct the orders of time and representation in fidelity to their necessary causal relations and to the rest of the laws and objects of the already known world.

In short, without a principle of causality—of a necessary and irreversible connection of events following a constant rule—there can be no objective time. Without objective time there wouldn't even be subjective time, with all its private associations and assemblage of subjective representations under the unity of one consciousness. Hence the validity of the principle of causality is a condition of the possibility of self-consciousness, and even of the individual's inner subjective world.

Kant admits, indeed insists, that the a priori principles do not penetrate the essence of the phenomena, their "interior" so to speak. The knowledge they provide is knowledge of *relations*, not of essences. To fully know a particular thing is equal to knowing all the relations in which it stands. No insight into some occult essence is available to us. This limitation also means that we cannot rationally explain *why* nature and natural objects exist, only *how* they exist and operate: what are the necessary relations that explain their movements, alterations, effects on other objects, and also their generation and perishing as *particular* phenomena. Last year's hurricane arose necessarily because x, y, z occurred, and subsided necessarily when these forces went off. Yet no necessity attaches to the existence of the world with all its hurricanes and other matters of fact. The notion of necessary existence is excluded by the Critique as part of "bad" metaphysics, and this exclusion puts a rational limit on our desires to know. Thus, matters of fact are necessary only *within* the world, as effects of immanent empirical causes. But the very existence of the world is merely factual and, in this sense, contingent and inexplicable.

Third Analogy—the principle of interaction (or community)—"all substances, insofar as they can be perceived in space as simultaneous, are in thoroughgoing interaction" (B256) ("community [i.e., interaction with one another]" [A211]).

A particular substance according to Kant is everything to which the power to act or exercise influence can be attributed. (The model is the "effective" type of cause.) The third analogy, which attributes interaction to all substances, is needed in order to make possible the existence of a single world and to express its unity in dynamic terms, as a system in which everything affects everything. There is little doubt that Kant aims at Newton's law of universal gravitation, to which this analogy offers a meta-empirical (or metaphysical) ground. But note that we still don't have here a law of gravitation in its material and quantitative sense. The principle does not inform us whether the reciprocal causation between all substances is attraction or repulsion, or even cosmic love (as some Renaissance scholars believed). To determine this we need experience; and we further need to apply mathematics to experience in order to establish the *formula* of Newtonian gravitation, which alone provides concrete knowledge of nature. Finally, in order to explain a specific phenomenon, such as the moon's motion around earth, the laws of gravitation must be applied to particular cases. These layers of perception, experiment, calculation, and application, joined to the pure a priori principle, can illustrate what Kant meant by the synthesis of knowledge.

(D) **The Postulates of Empirical Thinking** refer to the categories of modality—possibility, actuality, and necessity—taken in their transcendental rather than logical meaning. From the standpoint of formal logic, everything is possible that does not involve contradiction, whereas in a transcendental (or meta-empirical) view, only that which conforms to the a priori conditions of experience is possible, that is, only that which can assume a spatiotemporal form and be subject to the categories, the schemes, the transcendental principles, and the empirical laws of nature based upon them.

This also implies that only that which can appear in sense perception is possible. In this way the empiricist principle, according to which the sole origin of valid knowledge is sensation (outer and inner), is here promoted to a *transcendental* principle and given a priori status, as opposed to its arbitrary and unproven status in British empiricism. However, Kant abolishes the exclusivity of the test of sensation and reduces it to one of several ingredients—necessary, though far from sufficient—within the synthesis that builds objects.

Logical and Empirical Necessity

When the formal conditions of the possibility of experience (space, time, categories) and the material conditions (sensation) are realized, the result is objective necessity. As mentioned, this necessity is not logical but transcendental; it derives from fulfilling all the conditions of experience. Kant stresses that this necessity concerns only the *state* of things but not their very existence. Metaphysics cannot explain why there is a world with natural objects in it: this would transgress the bounds of reason. In its purely logical sense, the idea of necessary existence is fallacious, and should not be used in the misleading manner of Spinoza. There is no valid passage from a logical or conceptual analysis to actual being. Yet *within* the empirical world, assuming it exists as a matter of fact, the particular entities in space and time affect each other with empirical necessity, which results from the agreement of the sensations with nature's Transcendental Principles and the empirical laws they ground.

This empirical necessity is what Kant sought in the first part of the Critique, in response to Hume and other skeptics. Kant basically accepted the empiricists' argument that neither induction nor any other construction from sensations can yield necessary connections. The problem he faced was to ground a concept of empirical necessity (which may also be called "meta-empirical" or "transcendental"), that on one side strictly distinguishes itself from logical necessity, and on the other side overcomes the skeptics' concerns. He believed this was achieved in the Analytic through the notion of transcendental logic. Kant summarizes the result in the last part of the section on the Postulates of Empirical Thinking, which states that *whatever exists in conformity with both the formal and material conditions of experience is necessary in the empirical sense.*

Note that the same would apply to "actual" as defined in the second postulate. Indeed, there is a systematic redundancy between the second and third postulates. Everything in nature that has actuality has it by necessity; and an object that is not empirically necessary cannot exist at all. This is Kant's strict determinism that inheres in his concept of objectivity. Even so, perhaps for reasons of symmetry with the categories, Kant assigns separate postulates to empirical actuality and necessity, so the section of modality appears to have three postulates under it when in substance it has only two.

The Object as Phenomenon and the Enigmatic Transcendental X

The transcendental logic with its concept of empirical necessity has defined a new concept of object. Instead of the transcendent object of traditional realism, which is said to reside outside all knowledge, the Analytic puts forward the concept of the *object as phenomenon*—an empirical, immanent natural entity whose reality is defined only within the sphere of knowledge and is strictly restricted to it.

In edition A Kant asks: since all we have in our mind are representations, not things in themselves but phenomena (appearances), what are we to understand by the concept of an object that both *corresponds* to knowledge and thereby also *differs* from it? His answer: "it is easy to see that this object must be thought of only as something in general = X, since outside of our cognition we have nothing that we could set over against this cognition as corresponding to it" (A104). There have been many views about the nature of this enigmatic X, some of them mystical and speculative; but I think the phrase "something [*etwas*] in general" emphasizes that what is meant by the reality of objects as phenomena is not a specific and concrete set of features but the element of *thinghood* in general—that rigid and involuntary facticity that characterizes being as such. In other words, the Königsberg town hall is an object as phenomenon, but there is no "town hall in itself" hiding behind it. What endows the building with empirical reality is the domain of being as such in which it is situated, the being that faces us as the *non-I*, as a limiting necessity. A real object, by its concept, resists our attempt to think of it in any arbitrary way, since it possesses a factual necessity that forces itself on whatever we may think or say of that object. This is its thinghood or objectivity, the mark of its being an object. What is the origin of this limiting necessity? Traditional philosophy ascribes it to the object's being a thing in itself outside our mind, whereas Kant identifies the origin of the object's necessity and unity *within* the boundaries of the thinking mind. "Since we have to do only with the manifold of our representations, and that X which corresponds to them (the object), because it should be something distinct from all our representations, is nothing for us, [therefore] the unity that the object makes necessary can be nothing other than the formal unity of the consciousness in the synthesis of the manifold of representations" (A105). Thereby the necessity of the object is removed from the direct impact of sensation and assigned to the understanding. It is the understanding that introduces into our experience the objective necessity that imposes itself on all our cognitive statements. The enigmatic X remains nothing (*nichts*) for us, an empty concept and the element of necessity attached to sensation is replaced by the transcendental unity of self-consciousness as the barrier to arbitrary thinking.[22] Everything that conforms to the conditions of the unity of experience—to space and time, the categories, the schemes, the fundamental principles of nature, and the empirical laws that are based on them—would be an objective state of affairs, with which all specific cognitive judgments must conform, while also agreeing with each other with respect to it.[23]

In the *Prolegomena* (paras. 18–19) Kant explains his concept of objectivity by distinguishing two kinds of judgment: (a) *Judgments of perception* are empirical judgments that have only subjective authority and are valid only in relation to myself at a certain point of time.[24] (b) *Judgments of experience* are empirical judgments that have objective authority, that is, relation to an object, and are valid always and necessarily for everyone. This implies an inner link between objectivity and universality-cum-necessity. If the judgment is true of the object, it will agree with any other true judgment made of this object at any time by me or by anyone else; and vice versa: "when we have ground for considering a judgement as having necessarily universal validity . . . we must consider that it is objective also—that is, that it expresses not merely a reference of our perception to a subject, but a characteristic of the object" (para. 18). Objective validity

22. Actually, this is not even a concept, but a contentless sign of a concept.

23. Nevertheless, this empty X is an ontological sign that refers to a domain of being that cannot be approached or cognized. Kant ultimately ends with an unsolved ontological dualism, which raised much debate in German Idealism and beyond.

24. *Wahrnehmungsurteile*—judgments of sense perception.

and universal-cum-necessary validity are convertible concepts (para. 19), so once we have universal and necessary validity that fits the unity of experience, we thereby have a relation to an object without having to perform an impossible leap—indeed *a salto mortale*—outside the sphere and conditions of the knowing mind.

Kant names this empirical object "phenomenon" (appearance), but thereby, as I pointed out above, he does not mean a pale or partial copy or representation of some hidden original entity. A phenomenon is immanent to experience; as such it is real and complete in its kind and definition, an empirical reality in time and space. (Recall Kant's distinction between transcendental ideality and empirical reality above.) Indeed, two of the categories that constitute empirical objects are named—not in vain— reality and actuality. Reality indicates the involuntary aspect of sensation—an essential property of empirical entities—and actuality means that this entity underwent categorization and is coherently integrated in the rest of nature's law-governed processes within the one world of experience. These are new, theoretical definitions of veteran ontological concepts. The empirical object is not a thing in itself, since its reality depends on the synthesis of sensation, time, space, and the categories, all of which are the subject's a priori modes of operation. While the thing in itself—a problematic concept that Kant insisted on keeping, and which caused him a great deal of trouble—is said to have extraempirical reality, which as such is unfathomable and defies determination. As for the Kantian phenomenon, it represents only itself.[25]

The Refutation of Idealism

We mentioned that in edition B Kant added the section on the refutation of Idealism. He did this in order that his doctrine not

---

25. Kant's unfortunate choice of the Platonic idiom "appearance"—with its problematic connotations—shifts the issue to areas that Kant's substantive philosophy sought to leave behind.

be confused with that of Berkeley, who denied the existence of
space and matter, and also to argue against Descartes's view that
there can be a wordless subject, and a consciousness of a world
without entities.[26] Kant thinks of himself as a transcendental
idealist, but insists he remains an empirical realist. This is because the new philosophical interpretation he gave to space,
time, matter, and empirical being does not abolish their empirical reality and does not enclose the human being within the
confines of his or her private consciousness while negating the
world of objects outside. Berkeley admitted only the existence of
perceptions and perceivers, consciousness and their ideas, while
Kant argues that the perceiver, as owner of a stream of perceptions, would be impossible unless, opposing him, he confronts a
world that has a unity of its own, distinct from the private unity
of every particular consciousness. In other words, in order for
us to have a stream of subjective states of consciousness, there
must exist something objectively spatial outside us. This is again
the argument of the Transcendental Deduction, which here fo-
cuses on the issue of space (and indirectly, matter). Space is the
permanent anchor in relation to which there can be temporal
changes, and thus is the substrate of that external world in relation to which alone I can become conscious of myself. Hence, as
Kant summarized in a succinct sentence, "the consciousness of
my own existence is at the same time an *immediate* consciousness of the existence of other things outside me" (B276). It is
not a logical inference, but a simultaneous awareness. Hence,
in order to know with certainty that there is a world, we do not
have to leap outside our inner experience; on the contrary, we
must turn to this inner experience and explicate the phenomenological conditions for its possibility, realizing that "inner

26. Kant names three different types of Idealism: Dogmatic (Berkeley),
Problematic (Descartes), and Transcendental (his own). Kantian Idealism ac-
knowledges the empirical reality of the spatial world while rejecting the possibility of a worldless self.

experience itself is consequently only mediate and possible only through outer experience" (B277).[27]

In What Sense Is the Transcendental Logic Considered a Critical Metaphysics?

In conclusion of the Analytic we may pause to ask what Kant achieved in it in terms of his main program—to reconcile the metaphysical and the critical interests of reason. To this end we should consider in what way his theory of the transcendental (or synthetic) logic is metaphysical, and what makes it critical.

Under "metaphysics" two things have usually been understood: (a) searching for the supersensible foundations of the sensible world (nature); (b) explicating the meaning of being or existence in general. Both topics characterize Kant's transcendental logic. First, the ingredients of this logic, the categories and transcendental principles, are supersensible elements—determined a priori without depending on experience, but rather making experience depend on them—while at the same time determining the ground structure of the sensible world itself. These are factors beyond nature that shape a priori the image of nature itself and of the particular objects in it. As a result, getting to know the synthetic logic allows us to know something about the structure of nature and all its objects prior to observing them with our senses. For example, we know in advance that *if* there is a nature with entities in it, then all lend themselves to sensible observation, all are mathematically quantifiable, all are causes and effects in mechanistic-like sequences, all are substances or inhere in a substance, all stand in some reciprocal relations, and, of course, all exist in time and partly also in space. Moreover, from here one can derive further elements, concepts like motion, matter, change, and many others, which are equally

27. The two are not really immediate, but simultaneously mediate each other.

metaphysical in the same sense, although they are not primary like the categories; therefore Kant may call the complete body of knowledge that evolves from here a "metaphysics of nature" (as he did).[28]

Second, the synthetic (transcendental) logic taken as a whole, as a system of forms and conditions, constitutes an explication and a new interpretation of the concept of empirical existence. If we wish to know what it means for natural entities *to be*, or "to be an actual object," we shall find the answer in synthetic (transcendental) logic, which teaches that for natural objects to exist means to be given in sensation and fulfill all the conditions of temporality, spatiality, causality, and the rest of the supersensible principles discussed in the Analytic. To be sure, we pay an important price here: limiting our knowledge to the domain of empirical existence. This is not an explication of being in general, but only of the realm of empirical being that alone is open to human metaphysical understanding.

In these two senses Kant can see his doctrine as metaphysical. At the same time, this metaphysics is critical for two main reasons.

First, as a metaphysics of empirical being (or a metaphysics of experience, as it has been aptly called), it is confined to observable entities, and its components acquire meaning and validity only when applied to appropriate sense perceptions. This can be put also as follows: what we know of the objects in nature is conditional knowledge—the condition being that there is an empirical experience at all, and there are given sensations to which the metaphysical principles can be fittingly applied. In this respect, Kant's metaphysics observes the ground critical principle according to which there can be no determination of existence without empirical input.

---

28. As he did in the Critique, promising to develop this less urgent part of the system later, and started to do in his *Metaphysical Foundations of Natural Science*.

Second, the components of the synthetic logic refer not to supersensible *beings*, but only to supersensible *forms* or *patterns* that are invested in the building of the natural world. This logic in itself does not allow us to know any actual being, neither empirical nor superempirical, neither on earth nor in heaven; what we know are the superempirical *elements* that participate in the constitution of the empirical being and condition its possibility, elements that have no separate existence and receive their concrete meaning only from this constitutive role. Dogmatic metaphysics characteristically claims to determine the existence of beings of reason (*entia rationis*) outside experience, while critical metaphysics abstains from this attempt and determines only the functioning *within* experience of superempirical factors that shape and constitute experience itself. Thereby the former counts as transcendent metaphysics, and the latter as immanent.

The metaphysical role of Kant's synthetic logic is seen also from another angle. The Copernican principle states that the conditions of *knowing* actual objects in nature are equally the conditions of their *being* objects in nature. In other words, there are not two separate sets of conditions, but the conditions of knowledge and the conditions of existence of natural objects make one single system. That system, transcendental logic, is thus both epistemological and ontological, a doctrine both of the modes of knowing nature and of the modes of being an empirical object in nature.

Phenomena and Noumena

Kant closes the Analytic with a distinction between phenomena and noumena, appearances and intellectual entities. We have seen that Kant's choice of the term "phenomenon" is not meant to downgrade the objects of empirical knowledge as unreal. Rather, the synthesis by which these objects are constituted is subject to the categories of reality and actuality, and the term "phenomenon" refers to real natural objects as the objects of legitimate knowledge. (This is also the meaning of the empirical realism that Kant ascribes to himself.) Kant goes on to distinguish between a phenomenon in this sense and an arcane metaphysical being that cannot be known in principle, which he names here "noumenon" (i.e., a being of the intellect that cannot have any empirical features). Kant scholars debate whether noumenon and the thing in itself signify the same, but for present purposes it may suffice that both terms refer to a mode of being that can only be thought but not known. In other words, we may not attribute properties to it or speak of it in predicative statements, which attach predicates to it as their subject. All that such terms can do is point to some blank reality beyond nature, to which we cannot give any content and meaning. Kant constantly emphasizes that the categories can be applied only to phenomena and not to things in themselves. The failure to observe this fundamental rule leads to the delusions of the Dialectic. Nevertheless, speaking of noumena has a useful negative role, in marking the boundaries of a meaningful application of the categories and charting a realm we can never reach, although we endeavor and are tempted to do so. Kant summarizes: "In the end, however, we have no insight into the possibility of such noumena, and the domain outside of the sphere of appearances is empty (for us). . . . The concept of a noumenon is therefore merely a *boundary concept*, in order to limit the pretensions of sensibility, and therefore only of negative use. But it is nevertheless not invented arbitrarily, but is rather connected with the limitation of sensibility, yet without being able to posit anything positive outside of the domain of the latter" (A255/B310–11).[29]

---

29. While this is Kant's position in this chapter, it is hard to say that he remains always faithful to it. As a matter of fact, his oeuvre contains enough positive statements about this ineffable realm, that whoever collects them will be in a position to write an ironic dissertation titled "What Kant Knew of the Unknowable."

The Transcendental Dialectic

The noumena are objects of a metaphysical striving of reason that can be neither satisfied nor abolished. This is the broader theme of Division 2 of the transcendental logic, titled "Dialectic." Kant defines the Dialectic as "the logic of illusion." It is the invalid part of transcendental logic, namely, of metaphysics, of which the Critique exposes the delusions as well as their origin in reason itself. The logic of illusion pretends that reason by itself is capable of proving God's existence and the immortality of the soul, and to determine other matters that cannot in principle be subject to observation and measurement, like the freedom of the will and the boundaries of the universe. But unlike trivial or accidental errors, this is an inevitable illusion deriving from the very nature of rationality. Herein lies one of Kant's deepest and most interesting ideas concerning the nature of philosophy.

The Unconditioned as Totality

The critical metaphysics established by the Analytic is a metaphysics of finite and conditioned entities, and this in two senses: (1) they are conditioned by (depend upon) sense perception; (2) they determine each other in causal chains. Yet human reason, says Kant, has a necessary interest in the unconditioned—a drive toward the whole and the absolute. This is not a mere desire or emotional excitement, but a rational drive that exhibits the nature of rationality. To be rational is, among other things, to demand a ground and explanation for everything, including for every ground and explanation we have received in the previous stage. In principle, therefore, this demand cannot be satisfied until a total and absolute explanation has been reached. The fact that we strive to know the comprehensive reasons for the world's existence—that we ask questions about the world as a whole or search for the absolute and ultimate element in things—is therefore no caprice of an inquisitive mind but an essential element of human reason. Unfortunately, in being finite rational beings, we are unable to give that rational drive a response that would also be rational (at least not in the field of knowledge).

The Dialectic is the domain in which this kind of "big," absolute questions are deliberated and submitted to critical scrutiny. Following Spinoza—or at least, similar to his mode of thinking—Kant translates the concept of absolute, or the unconditioned, into the concept of *totality*. The unconditioned is the comprehensive and total field of discussion, because it is supposed to contain everything within itself, including the relevant explanation of itself. As the drive toward the absolute takes the form of a drive toward totality, we raise questions about the cosmos as a whole, about God as the most comprehensive real being, and about the soul as the presumed substance holding together the totality of one's mental actions and states.

In this way Kant gives a rational interpretation, in terms of his system, to the grand questions of classical metaphysics and theology: Is there a god? Is the soul immortal? Does the cosmos, when viewed as a single whole, have a beginning in time? In space? Does it leave room for freedom? For miracles? Is matter made of atoms or is it rather indefinitely divisible? Is there, within or without the chains of natural (external) causes, a supercause that exists necessarily?

The Ideas of Reason

Kant assembles these questions into three "ideas of pure reason": the psychological idea (the soul), the cosmological idea (the world), and the theological idea (God). By "idea" he means not every ordinary mental content, as did Descartes and the British empiricists, but an extraordinary or sublime concept formed in the shape of a totality, which rises above the empirical realm and is completely inapplicable to it. Reason by its nature produces those ideas necessarily, yet they have almost always led to fallacious and misleading results in philosophy and religion.

The transcendental dialectic analyzes the flaws in the common use of these ideas, and shows in detail how their core fallacy branches off into specific flaws in our thinking. Finally, it asks whether there is a way of transforming the ideas into immanent, and critically legitimate, instruments of science.

In terms of Kant's system, the origin of the ideas lies in the tension between the conditioned and the unconditioned, and the typical fallacy we commit consists in the false, but unavoidable, inference from the former to the latter, to wit, that if the conditioned is given, then the whole series of conditions that had determined it, and thereby the unconditioned, is also given.

Kant would agree that if the conditioned is given, then the *concept* of the unconditioned is given with it, namely, the concept of the whole series of preceding conditions—as well as the *drive* toward it; but the total series is not thereby actually given. As finite rational beings we can only move *within* the series of conditioned items, passing from one finite synthesis to another (that is, from one segment of experience to another)—without ever reaching the full totality to which our striving is oriented.

Before presenting a bird's-eye view of Kant's main argument, two preliminary notes are in order. First, Kant does not refute the soul's immortality, the existence of God, and the actuality of freedom. He only refutes the possibility to prove them by pure cognitive reason. The result is not negation but indetermination.

Second, since the ideas, by definition, are not applicable to the senses, Kant declares that their only valid application is to the "understanding." By this he means not the pure categories and principles as such, but their *products* in the different empirical sciences. The ideas do not serve to constitute an object; their role is to add further, second-level forms of organization and systematic unity (such as genus and species, or links between disciplines) to the empirical objects that have already been constituted by the scientific understanding; and they are meant to offer systematic unity to the partial views of the universe that the ongoing work of synthesis has already produced (see later, the section on the Regulative Idea).

The Immortality of the Soul: The Paralogisms

Dogmatic metaphysics (including Enlightenment thinkers before Kant) believed it possible to demonstrate the soul's immortality by reason alone. The core argument was that the soul is given to us in self-consciousness as a simple substance, which as such is neither divisible nor perishable. Kant examines the positions of several philosophers from Descartes to Mendelssohn, and finds they share a common flaw. His main argument: one must not confuse the function of the *logical subject* with the *real* subject of thinking. "**I Think**' is thus the sole text of rational psychology, from which it is to develop its entire wisdom" (A343/B401). Yet this text contains very poor information concerning ontology (indeed, none), and one cannot extract from it any real being, certainly not a substance. Substance is a metaphysical category that we introduce illegitimately—indeed, smuggle—into the consciousness "I think." What is given in the Cartesian *cogito* is not a real being but only a basic form of thought, to which the ontological interpretations attach arbitrary additions. The pure ego is a logical-mental function that works as the highest form of our representations. All our thoughts and representations must stand in relation to it in order to be possible, and in order for us to think or experience anything at all. Yet as such it is not a being of any kind, neither empirical nor superempirical (metaphysical), but a mere form of the subject—a form whose functions and modes of operation we may investigate in detail (as we did in the deduction of the categories), but we may not reify the form of subjectivity into a special metaphysical substance.

In short, philosophers like Descartes, Leibniz, and Mendelssohn presume to extract from the mere form of the pure ego ontological information that it does not and cannot contain;

and this illegal passage creates "paralogisms" in reason, that is, deluding inferences and insights. On the other side, however, every person as a natural being does have an *empirical* soul (or ego), which is an observable phenomenon in time. To Kant, the empirical soul is a real psychological object in nature; one can observe its behavior, and organize its states and history using the categories and the laws of experimental psychology. Such an investigation uses the category of substance legitimately to unify a plurality of inner intuitions in time; but then the object of this study is not the pure transcendental ego that accompanies every thought, but the empirical mind of some person. The latter is a natural object like any other, a finite entity subject to time, which has been created by natural causes and is due to perish. If we also have an eternal noumenal soul is a question the Critique cannot answer.

The Antinomies: The World as Totality

Kant attempts to summarize the classic paradoxes of rationalism since Zeno of Elea in four questions: Does the world have boundaries in time and space? Is there a limit to the divisibility of matter? Is everything in the world absolutely determined, or is there room for freedom too? Is there a necessary being inside or outside the world that acts as its cause? Each of these questions, in being directed to the world as thing in itself, produces two contradictory answers, a thesis and an antithesis, each of which can be proved by refuting its opposite, and thus a self-contradiction is exhibited in reason.

Earlier in this book I mentioned the meaning of the term "antinomy" in Kant. An antinomy is a pair of contradictory statements (a "thesis" and an "antithesis"), each of which can, apparently, be demonstrated by the ground principles of one and the same rational system. The cosmological idea—the idea of the world as the totality of all phenomena—gives rise to antinomies, because it makes claims about the world as a single whole and as a thing in itself, although such a totality is never given to us and cannot exist in our experience. The only experience we have concerns some segment, part, or aspect of the world. And while it certainly can crystallize into causal and scientific knowledge of this segment, it always remains partial and marked by finitude. Our empirical world is woven from such segments of objectivized experience, in which conditioned entities and events point back to other conditioned entities and events that preceded them in an open-ended series that never reaches the unconditioned totality. Hence, the Critique states boldly that "the world does not exist at all (independently of the regressive series of my representations); it exists . . . only in the empirical regress of the series of appearances, and by itself it is not to be met with at all" (A505/B533). However, the dialectical illusion raises questions about the world in itself existing independently of the series of experiences (like "has the world a beginning in time?"), which throws reason into a tangle of contradictions.

To Kant it is clear that an inner contradiction in the system of reason is utterly impossible. Hence, something must be basically defective in the arguments that seem to have produced it—a defect that, nevertheless, can be removed by critical deliberation. This deliberation stands on two pillars of critical reason: the strict distinction between phenomena and things in themselves, and the rigorous principle that limits the application of the categories (and the other a priori elements) to phenomena alone. By means of these principles Kant reaches the conclusion that the first two antinomies (which he dubs "mathematical," because they deal with quantity) are based on meaningless concepts; therefore their resolution consists in abolishing the very question as void. In the case of the two other antinomies (dubbed "dynamic," because they deal with causality) both the thesis and antithesis *might* be true, each in a different domain: one in the phenomenal domain and one in the noumenal.

More specifically, when asking if the world as such has boundaries in space and time, or if its matter can be divided

endlessly, one demands an account in mathematical terms—
the terms of the forms of intuition—of an entity that is not empirical and cannot be given in time and intuition. This mode
of thinking has produced over the centuries paradoxes that
reason is unable to resolve, and in fact commits an error *in
the very asking*. The fallacy results from ascribing temporal
and spatial properties to things in themselves. To ask about
the beginning of the world is similar to studying the properties
of a round quadrangle or wondering if a triangle tastes good.
Whatever our answer, we have said nothing at all. In the end,
Kant expects that the proponents of the thesis and the antithesis, having refuted each other endlessly to no avail, will realize
"they are disputing about nothing," and that "a certain transcendental illusion has portrayed a reality to them where none
is present" (A501/B529–30). The antinomy is resolved, then,
by dismissing the question with its two conflicting answers as
meaningless.

While the mathematical antinomies are resolved by abolishing the very question at their base, the resolution of the dynamic
(causal) antinomies allows the two sides to reach a kind of coex-
istence, in which the thesis and antithesis might both be true—
each in a different ontological domain. This, too, calls for a distinction between phenomena and things in themselves. Thus,
the question about determinism and the freedom of the will can
be approached from a dual point of view. On the one hand, a
human action, as an event in the empirical world, is a member of a series of natural causes that determine it. On the other
hand, there is nothing to exclude the possibility that, at the same
time, it *might* also derive from a noumenal causality outside the
series. Whether this is actually the case we shall never know, but,
Kant argues, at least it is not a priori impossible. This dualist
solution, which gave rise to different objections and interpretations, cannot be construed as if Kant suggests there is in fact a
freedom of the will. All Kant is willing to say is that we can think
meaningfully and without contradiction of a noumenal aspect of

reality that possesses a causality of its own and exists alongside the empirical aspect.[30]

Note that, thereby, an asymmetry is set between the antithesis, which refers to the phenomenal world and is accepted as unquestionably true, and the thesis, which concerns a presumed hidden world and remains problematic and lacking a cognitive decision (a *moral* decision will be offered in Kant's ethical theory).

God's Existence

Kant classifies all the proofs of God's existence in three basic paradigms: an ontological proof, a cosmological proof, and a physico-theological proof. If all three were refuted, this would spell the end of all attempts to prove God's existence by means of pure reason. In addition, Kant identifies the footprints of the ontological proof—which deduces God's existence from his concept—in the other two paradigmatical proofs, which turns the ontological proof into the main target of his attack.

(1) **The ontological proof** has medieval precedents in the work of St. Anselm. Renewed in early modernity by Descartes, Spinoza, and Leibniz, it became characteristic of precritical rationalism. All versions of this proof share in common a direct, a priori passage from God's concept (essence) to his existence. Spinoza speaks of the divine substance as "that whose essence includes existence" (*Ethics* I axiom 1), and Descartes declares that God's existence follows from his essence just as it follows from the essence of the triangle that its three angles equal two

---

30. Kant adds a further reservation to his position: "We have not even tried to prove the **possibility** of freedom; for this would not have succeeded either, because from mere concepts a priori we cannot cognize anything about the possibility of any real ground or any causality. . . . [To show] that this antinomy rests on a mere illusion, and that nature at least **does not conflict with** causality through freedom—that was the one single thing we could accomplish, and it alone was our sole concern" (A558/B586).

right angles (*Meditations*, chap. 5). In a variation on Anselm, Descartes states that God, by his essence, possesses all perfections, and since existence is a perfection, God would be lacking a perfection if he did not exist; so God exists necessarily. Kant sets out not against a specific version of the ontological argument but against the mode of thinking at its ground, which deduces existence from concepts. This mode of thinking is the core of dogmatic metaphysics and the direct opposite of the critical principle. The question "what is there?" cannot be answered by mere conceptual analysis. If it refers to empirical entities, then the concept should be joined with the relevant sense perception, and if it refers to entities outside experience, we have no way to know and should abstain from judgment.

More specifically, the ontological proof fails in that it conceives existence to be one of a thing's *properties*. But existence is not a property, says Kant; existence is a metaphysical status that can be added or not added to some subject without change in its properties. When we state that x (say, a coin) is round, shining, and gilded, we attribute to it properties or link its concept with predicates. But when we say of x that it exists, we do not add a new property to it, but situate it with all its properties in the domain of existence. One must not confuse such situating (in Kant's words, *Setzen* [positing]) with predication. The difference between an existing hundred dollars and a nonexisting hundred dollars is not a difference in a predicate or property; rather, it is the very *same* hundred dollars, with the *same* properties, that we think to be present in one case and absent in the other. If existence were a property, I would be changing the properties of anything I conceive as existing—and thus would not be conceiving *it*, but already something else. Hence the ontological proof is void of ontological content, and the properties it analytically ascribes to God remain confined within the concept. All we can say is that *if* there were a God, he would have possessed all the properties that follow from his concept; but that *indeed* there is a God cannot be deduced from this. Kant concludes with a touch of ridicule: "Thus the famous ontological (Cartesian) proof . . . is so much trouble and labor lost, and a human being can no more become richer in insight from mere ideas than a merchant could in resources if he wanted to improve his financial state by adding a few zeroes to his cash balance" (A602/B630).

If we take a deeper look we can realize that Kant rejects the very notion of a necessary being as unintelligible. Being is not inherently necessary; it is endowed with necessity from outside, by the network of relations, causal and others, in which one being stands to other beings, whose necessity is equally drawn from their relations with their predecessors and from the system as a whole. Hence being itself is contingent, and there is no conceptual way to explain or explicate it, nor the ultimate facticity and being-so that marks it. Being, Kant seems to hold, can only be *encountered*, affirmed, or negated as a rigid datum; and for human beings, he insists, this occurs only by means of intuition. Where no intuition is possible, one cannot posit being; and doing so by rational thinking alone is a tempting but deluded venture.

(2) **The cosmological proof** starts from the existence of some finite and conditioned being (for example, I myself), and infers from here there must exist also an absolutely necessary being. Apparently, here we have a proof based on experience and not on a merely conceptual analysis. But Kant argues that soon the cosmological argument bids farewell to experience and resumes the ontological mode of reasoning. Experience leads only to the *concept* of a necessary being, but not to a necessary being that *actually* exists. Therefore, in order to pass from the concept to the actual thing, one turns again to the analysis of concepts and asks, the concept of which entity corresponds to the concept of necessary existence and allows to deduce it; and when finding that this is the concept of *ens realissimum*, the most real being, namely, God, one concludes that God exists necessarily. Yet thereby, Kant polemicizes, one is clearly presupposing that the mere *concept* of *ens realissimum* is sufficient as ground

for deducing an absolute necessity of existence, and this is no other than the principle of the ontological proof that we wanted to avoid (A607/B635). In this way (and others that cannot be spelled out here) Kant argues that the cosmological proof tacitly contains the ontological proof and is likewise invalid.[31]

Kant's dry discussions of these topics sometimes make room for the intense existential experience behind them:

> The unconditioned necessity, which we need as indispens- ably as the ultimate sustainer of all things, is for human reason the true abyss. Even eternity—however awful the sublimity with which a Haller might portray it[32]—does not make such a dizzying impression on the mind; for eternity only **measures** the duration of things, but it does not **sus- tain** that duration. One cannot resist the thought of it, but one also cannot bear it that a thing we represent to ourselves as the highest among all possible beings might, as it were, say to itself : "I am from eternity to eternity; outside me is nothing except what is something merely through my will; **but whence** then am I?" Here everything gives way beneath us, and the greatest perfection as well as the smallest, hovers without support before speculative reason (for which it would cost nothing to let the one as much as the other disap- pear without the least obstacle). (A613/B641)

Kant's verdict is that "unconditioned necessity, which we need as indispensably as the ultimate sustainer of all things, is for

---

31. Actually, Kant could disprove the cosmological proof with the argument that the conditioned being can lead us only to the concept of the unconditioned, but not to its reality; or, to put it differently (while relying on the broader argu- ment of the Dialectic), because we are always inside a series that passes, end- lessly, from one conditioned to another. But that was not enough for Kant, who wished to demolish the concept of "necessary being" and show it is so elusive that it can be found hiding in many different false ideas.

32. Haller was a naturalist and philosophical poet who described the mind's awe before the vastness of the open universe, the limitlessness of time, and the experience of vertigo of senses and thought that it invokes.

human reason the true abyss" (A613/B641). And this is equally true of the notion of necessary being: not that we do not know if something like that exists—the very notion is void.

(3) **The physico-theological proof** (the proof from design) starts from the impressive manifestation of wisdom, purpose, beauty, and adaptability that are to be found in nature and arouse our wonder and admiration—and proceeds to infer that there must be an infinite and wise world creator who planned and produced all these wonders. Actually this is a variety of the cosmological proof, but whereas the latter starts from a finite creature in general—*any* finite being—the physico-theological proof starts from *special* signs in nature that seemingly allude to the Supreme Being at their origin. Kant considers this the most natural and unsophisticated proof, with the greatest power of attraction; yet it is as fallacious as its two predecessors. This is because in part it tacitly relies on these predecessors, and partly due to a specific flaw of its own. The latter is the analogic and anthropomorphic mode of thinking, which regards those phenomena in analogy to human products and thus "does violence to nature and constrains it not to proceed in accordance with its own ends but to bend to ours (the similarity of nature's ends to houses, ships and clocks)" (A626/B654). Furthermore, the analogy with human products refers only to the *form* that is taking shape in nature but not to its matter and substance; so that even if it had been valid, it would at most have been able to prove a world *architect* but not a world *creator* (A627/B655).

As in the cosmological proof, Kant's argument distinguishes two stages: the stage of overflowing wonder, and the attempt to conceptualize it in a rational argument. The first stage starts from a real experience, the second repeats the fallacy of passing from the *concept* of contingency to the actual existence of a necessary being. The second stage stresses the accidental character attributed to purposive phenomena from the standpoint of the universal laws of nature, which are exclusively causal and mechanistic. But first, there is no evidence that nature cannot produce such systems by its own resources and laws,[33] and second, the physico-theological proof reiterates the fallacious procedure known from its predecessors:

> After one has gone as far as admiring the magnitude of the wisdom, power, etc., of the world's author, and cannot get any farther, then one suddenly leaves this argument which is based on empirical grounds . . . and goes back to the contingency that was inferred right at the beginning from the world's order and purposiveness. Now from this contingency alone [as our only presupposition], and solely through transcendental concepts, one [1] proceeds to the existence of something absolutely necessary, and then [2] goes on and passes to the concept of an all-encompassing reality. Thus the physico-theological proof that got stuck in the middle of its mission suddenly jumps over to the cosmological proof, and as the latter is only a concealed ontological proof, it follows that, in truth, the physico-theological proof actually carried out its aim through pure reason only. (A629/B657; I slightly changed the Guyer-Wood translation)

In the end, since it is impossible to prove God's existence either from pure concepts or from experience, the horizon for a *cognitive* demonstration is blocked, and rational theology aborts and lands on the rocks. Henceforth, the following two Critiques (of pure practical reason and of the power of judgment) and the book on religion within the confines of reason alone, will put forward a concept of a *moral* theology based on the decrees of the *human* will and on the historical project of this will, as analyzed at length in my *Kant and the Philosophy of History* (Princeton, 1980, 1989).

It is noteworthy that unlike his sneering attitude toward the ontological proof, Kant had great respect for the elating

---

33. A similar claim was made by Spinoza (see *Ethics* III, proposition 2, scholium).

experience prompted by the purposive phenomena in the universe—an experience not dissimilar to that of the sublime—and searched for ways of using teleology in a critical mode, neither making the concept of end a constitutive category, nor assuming a necessary world creator on its account. These attempts led to the third Critique's uncommon concept of "purposiveness without a purpose."

The Regulative Idea

The critique of reason in the negative sense refuted reason's ability to draw from itself a rationalist theory of the soul (psychology), of the world (cosmology), and of God (theology). The adjective "rationalist" is used in this context negatively, as knowledge derived from reason alone without the participation of the senses; hence, from a critical viewpoint the positions promoted by these alleged "rational" sciences are rather irrational. Does this mean that the concept of totality that underlies the Dialectic has no positive use? Kant's answer: no, there is a positive use, but it is *regulative* and not constitutive. The various concepts of totality cannot take part in the constitution of the objective world, yet they have a vital role in marking the open-ended horizons that call for the unending extension of our empirical knowledge of the immanent world, and the deepening of its systematic coherence.

In other words, we cannot know the totality of the world as a single transcendent thing; we can know only specific empirical phenomena *within* the world—to weave together portions of our scientific experience so as to make larger and more intensely coherent compounds. The regulative idea calls upon reason to never make do with partial, fragmentary results, but always strive to know further areas and aspects of the world: more causes and effects, new natural laws, and more continuous links between the natural laws and natural species we already know. This is a genuinely rational norm, which had strayed into the wrong path of pursuing transcendent, supernatural entities, but the regulative idea reverts it to the immanent world and directs it toward the infinitely open horizons of empirical research. Thus the metaphysical interest, expressed as a striving for totality and infinity, is rechanneled into a valid and fruitful course. The regulative idea deals with the products of the scientific understanding, which it seeks to endow with second-order patterns of order, organization, and classification that do not affect the constitutions of objects but allow for more unity, continuity, and affinity between the separate domains of science (physics, chemistry, biology, geology, etc.),[34] between the various natural laws, and between the many species and genera discovered in nature.

The regulative idea is a kind of inner imperative of science, which sets itself a dual objective: to *extend* scientific knowledge into new areas and regions, and to *intensify* the systematic texture of the already obtained bodies of knowledge, by connecting scientific disciplines and natural species, and by offering "thicker" causal explanations based on new facts and laws. (In latter-day terms one may cite the example of Einstein's attempts to unify the basic physical forces in the universe, or current attempts to give biology a foot in chemistry.) Kant's actual picture of science was limited by the sciences of his day, yet his regulative idea is still stirring in scientific work today and invoking debates in the philosophy of science.

In these debates, Kant's position would be characterized today as conservative. Like Spinoza before and Einstein later, Kant was guided by the vision of a single, all-inclusive coherent science. The regulative idea sets this semi-monotheistic vision within the immanent world, as the ultimate, never-to-be-attained goal of human knowledge. Thereby it performs a crucially important critical move; yet some would argue that this goal presents an overly harmonistic picture of rationality, and therefore is still

34. Today we can add also biochemistry, genetics, neurophysiology, etc.

tainted by marks of dogmatism. However, this is a broader issue in Kant. The philosopher of critical reason was not, perhaps, radical enough in exposing its limitations; but he shaped the way and signaled its philosophical and spiritual advantage.

Metaphysical Tension and Self-Knowledge

Indeed, if we are to summarize the mental results of Kant's dialectic beyond its technical and logical apparatus, we might say that the inner tension it generates awakens in the philosophizing mind the self-consciousness of its finitude. On the one hand, the metaphysical interest is an interest of reason itself. Even when directed to the big and eternal questions, about which no critical metaphysics is possible, one must view the very questioning, the wonder, the striving for transcendent objects, as *rational* activity. Yet on the other, this limitless drive generates irrational error and contradictions. The attempts to silence such questioning or "cure" the mind of it (as some positivist philosophies have suggested, even in Kant's own name)—or to abandon reason altogether in favor of answers offered by intuition, desire, a sense of need, a leap of faith, the power of tradition, or various forms of mystical revelation—would equally have to be judged as irrational. The genuine rational position demands that the great metaphysical questions be recognized as meaningful and necessary even while critical reason determines they are unanswerable. The other two alternatives—to ignore and repress the questions, or to offer them consoling, illusory answers—are two forms of unreason.[35]

35. Kant's famous statement in the preface to B, "I had to deny **knowledge** in order to make room for **faith**" (Bxxx), has long been misunderstood (as it was possibly meant to be). In this prudent declaration, Kant was using "faith" equivocally, both in its ordinary meaning as a religious attachment, and in the special meaning of his own theory of "rational faith," a noncognitive stance of practical reason that informs the moral will but is not to be understood as supporting irrational belief.

For Kant, reason is finite, yet only reason has valid authority. Both these statements are equally crucial. What reason cannot provide or confirm cannot be in our possession, while recognizing the finitude of reason is not only a rational way to live but even, perhaps, also a foundation of wisdom.

The classical ideal of wisdom was based on mental harmony resulting from knowing the highest truths. The ideal of wisdom of Kant's modern person would be to realize the consciousness of one's finitude and the rationality it entails—to know it is the *tension* between the meaningful questions and their impossible answers that defines the authentic human condition, and to make this recognition a defining force in one's life.

The dimension of transcendence does not disappear from the life of a critical philosopher. On the contrary, it hovers over it as a perennial issue, a horizon that is both significant and impenetrable, against which we live our finitude. The temptation to hear voices coming from this void, to communicate with it, or to leap beyond its threshold riding on a heartfelt mystical faith, will be resisted. Of course, this would leave a hiatus, a permanent fissure between the desired object and its fulfillment, and this indeed is a natural outcome of the critical self-awareness, which preserves the element of *eros* within the Kantian *logos* even at its highest achievement, and indeed as *part* of that achievement.

In conclusion, the inevitable relation to transcendence, and its critical redirection back to the immanent domain, signified a reflective knowledge—and thereby, the realization—of who we are and where we stand in being. The Critique with both its faces, the positive and the limiting, the driving and the restraining, is an indirect fulfillment of the ancient command "know thyself" by means of speech and by means of silence, by asserting capability and by accepting finitude.

SELECT BIBLIOGRAPHY

STUDIES ON KANT'S *Critique* abound. Some of them differ considerably—in scope, interpretation, clarity, level of detail, and attention to the historical context. The following list, citing some classic and contemporary studies, illustrates this diversity.

Allais, Lucy. *Manifest Reality: Kant's Idealism and His Realism.* Oxford: Oxford University Press, 2015.

Allison, Henry E. *Kant's Transcendental Idealism: An Interpretation and Defense.* New Haven, CT: Yale University Press, 1983.

Ameriks, Karl. *Kant's Theory of Mind: An Analysis of the Paralogisms of Pure Reason.* Oxford: Clarendon, 1982.

Bennett, Jonathan. *Kant's Analytic.* Cambridge: Cambridge University Press, [1966] 2016.

Burnham, Douglas, and Harvey Young, *Kant's "Critique of Pure Reason."* Edinburgh University Press, 2007.

Buroker, Jill Vance. *Kant's "Critique of Pure Reason": An Introduction.* Cambridge: Cambridge University Press, 2006.

Deleuze, Gilles. *Kant's Critical Philosophy: The Doctrine of the Faculties.* Translated by Hugh Tomlinson and Barbara Habberjam. London: Athlone Press, 1984.

Dickerson, A. B. *Kant on Representation and Objectivity.* Cambridge: Cambridge University Press, 2003.

Ewing, A. C. *A Short Commentary on Kant's "Critique of Pure Reason."* Chicago: University of Chicago Press, 1938.

Ferrarin, Alfredo. *The Powers of Pure Reason: Kant and the Idea of Cosmic Philosophy.* Chicago: University of Chicago Press, 2015.

Gardner, Sebastian. *Kant and the "Critique of Pure Reason."* London: Routledge, 1999.

Guyer, Paul, ed. *Cambridge Companion to Kant.* 2nd rev. ed. Cambridge: Cambridge University Press, 2006.

———, ed. *Cambridge Companion to Kant's "Critique of Pure Reason."* Cambridge: Cambridge University Press, 2010.

———. *Kant.* London: Routledge, 2006.

———. *Kant and the Claims of Knowledge.* Cambridge: Cambridge University Press, 1987.

Hahn, Robert. *Kant's Newtonian Revolution in Philosophy.* Carbondale: Southern Illinois University Press, 1988.

Hanna, Robert. *Kant and the Foundations of Analytic Philosophy*. Oxford: Clarendon, 2004.

Heidegger, Martin. *Phenomenological Interpretation of Kant's "Critique of Pure Reason."* Translated by Parvis Emad and Kenneth Maly. Bloomington: Indiana University Press, 1997.

Kemp Smith, Norman. *A Commentary to Kant's Critique of Pure Reason*. New York: Humanities Press, 1962.

Kitcher, Patricia, ed. *Kant's "Critique of Pure Reason": Critical Essays*. Lanham, MD: Rowman & Littlefield, 1998.

Longuenesse, Béatrice. *Kant and the Capacity to Judge: Sensitivity and Discursivity in the Transcendental Analytic of the "Critique of Pure Reason."* Princeton, NJ: Princeton University Press, 1998.

Paton, H. J. *Kant's Metaphysic of Experience: A Commentary on the First Half of the "Kritik der reinen Vernunft."* London: G. Allen & Unwin, 1970.

Penelhum, Terence, and J. J. MacIntosh, eds. *The First Critique: Reflections on Kant's "Critique of Pure Reason."* Belmont, CA: Wadsworth, 1969.

Pinkard, Terry. *German Philosophy, 1760–1860: The Legacy of Idealism*. Cambridge: Cambridge University Press, 2002.

Pippin, Robert. *Kant's Theory of Form: An Essay on the "Critique of Pure Reason."* New Haven, CT: Yale University Press, 1982.

Strawson, Peter F. *The Bounds of Sense: An Essay on Kant's "Critique of Pure Reason."* London: Routledge, 1966.

Van Cleve, James. *Problems from Kant*. New York: Oxford University Press, 1999.

Weldon, T. D. *Introduction to Kant's "Critique of Pure Reason."* Oxford: Clarendon, 1946.

Wilkerson, T. E. *Kant's "Critique of Pure Reason": A Commentary for Students*. Oxford: Clarendon, 1976.

Wood, Allen. *Kant*. Oxford: Blackwell, 2004.

4; the regulative idea and, 101–3; special interests of, 18–19

receptivity: sensation and, 9; spontaneity and, union of, 69–70

recognition/re-cognition, synthesis of, 54

refutation of Idealism, 66–67, 82–84

regressive argument of the Transcendental Deduction, 33–34, 46–51

regulative idea, 101–3

representations (*Vorstellungen*), 2–3, 9; "I think" and, 56–60, 63; of space, 31–33

reproduction, synthesis of, 53–54

Russell, Bertrand, 27n

schematism, 10, 67–70

scholastics, the: as dogmatists, 11; inference of existence from concepts, 19

science: explaining the possibility of, 48–51; natural (*see* natural sciences); the regulative idea and, 102

self-consciousness: finitude of, metaphysical tension and, 103–4; the "I" as transcendental, 65–66; "I think" as, 63, 91; "I think," conditions of the possibility of, 55–62; as source of human understanding, 49; synthesis as a function of, 40

self-knowledge, metaphysical tension and, 103–4

senses/sensation: the intellect as distinct from, 8–10; intensity of, the anticipations of perception and, 72; intuition and, 29–31; understanding and, 2, 9–10

skepticism, 10–14

soul: immortality of, paralogisms and, 91–92; the psychological idea and, 89

space: human subject, dependence on, 35–36, 83; intuition, as form of, 30, 64; intuition, representation as an, 33; Kant and his predecessors on, 32–33; objectivization of the orders of, 61; a priori character of, 31–32; regressive argument for the ideality of, 33–34; time and, asymmetry between, 34–35

Spinoza, Baruch: deductive-geometrical model championed by, 46n; dual opposition of Kant to, 4; nature's ability to produce by its own resources and laws, claim regarding, 100n; necessary existence, misleading use of, 78; the ontological proof of God's existence renewed by, 95; substantive knowledge as prior to knowing the method of knowledge, 5; totality, concept of the absolute translated into the concept of, 89

spontaneity: the intellect and, 8; receptivity and, union of, 69–70

subjective deduction, 52n

synthesis: of apprehension, 52–53, 64n; the hierarchy of syntheses, 52–55; idealist interpretation of, 40; as judgment, 41–45; of recognition/re-cognition, 54; of reproduction, 53–54; transcendental, 55; understanding and, 40, 45

synthetic judgments: analytic judgments and, distinction between, 23–25; mathematical propositions as, 25–27; in the natural sciences, 27–28; primary apparatus of a priori, 71 (*see also* Transcendental Principles)

synthetic logic. *See* transcendental logic

theological idea, 89. *See also* God's existence

A NOTE ON THE TYPE

THIS BOOK has been composed in Miller, a Scotch Roman typeface designed by Matthew Carter and first released by Font Bureau in 1997. It resembles Monticello, the typeface developed for The Papers of Thomas Jefferson in the 1940s by C. H. Griffith and P. J. Conkwright and reinterpreted in digital form by Carter in 2003.

Pleasant Jefferson ("P. J.") Conkwright (1905–1986) was Typographer at Princeton University Press from 1939 to 1970. He was an acclaimed book designer and AIGA Medalist.

The ornament used throughout this book was designed by Pierre Simon Fournier (1712–1768) and was a favorite of Conkwright's, used in his design of the *Princeton University Library Chronicle*.